THE STORY OF
ICKENHAM

By
Morris W. Hughes

Edited by
Brian Williams

HILLINGDON BOROUGH LIBRARIES
1983

Reprint 1992

© London Borough of Hillingdon 1983.
ISBN 0 907869 04 1
Designed by the London Borough of
Hillingdon Publicity Section
and printed by Echo Press (1983) Ltd., Loughborough
for Hillingdon Borough Libraries,
High Street, Uxbridge, Middlesex.

CONTENTS

List of Illustrations	5
Editor's Introduction	7
CHAPTER 1. BEFORE 1066 Stone Age and Iron Age finds at Harefield – An ancient earthwork in Ickenham? – The Romans – Saxon Landowners.	9
CHAPTER 2. NORMAN LORDS AND THEIR SUCCESSORS Domesday Book – The four local manors – The Clarkes.	12
CHAPTER 3. SWAKELEYS: THE MANOR AND THE HOUSE The De Swalclyves – The Shorediches – Sir Robert Vyner and Pepys – The Gilbey family – The old manor house – The architecture of Swakeleys	17
CHAPTER 4. THE CHURCHES St. Giles' architecture – Its bells and monuments – The parish registers – Nonconformity – The Bricketts – The chapel in the High Road – Later developments.	29
CHAPTER 5. LAW AND DISORDER Religious penalties – The constable – The court baron – The parish council – Dissidents and deviants – Roger Crab – A modern hermit – Tramps.	43
CHAPTER 6. PHILANTHROPY AND EDUCATION The Gell Bequest – The Pump – Early schools in Ickenham – Later developments.	52
CHAPTER 7. LEISURE AND PLEASURE The fair – The postmaster and the gypsies – Shooting at Swakeleys – A slide show – The debating society – The village hall – Sports.	65
CHAPTER 8. BLACKSMITHS AND BALLOONS The work of the smith – The first forge – The Montagues and Llewellyn Wood – The allotments – Common land – A balloon in 1913.	76

CHAPTER 9. AN ERA OF CHANGE   83
Impact of World War I – Joe Dickens' story – A fire – An aerial
bomb – Arthur Winch's story – War ends – Early railway days –
Metroland – The village burgeons – Modern times.

READING LIST   92

INDEX   92

ILLUSTRATIONS

Ickenham area from John Rocque's map of Middlesex, 1754	8
Home Farm about 1900	14
Manor Farm 1960	15
Swakeleys from an engraving of 1800	18
Swakeleys, 1819	21
Swakeleys – a modern view	22
Swakeleys about 1910	24-25
The Great Chamber, Swakeleys	27
The Font, St. Giles' Church	30
St. Giles' Church 1807, showing the old 'Buntings' at left	33
Ickenham Hall	34
St. Giles' Church about 1900	35
Effigy of the Clayton baby	36
The United Reformed Church	40
Ickenham showing the 'Coach and Horses' about 1910	44
Roger Crab, the Ickenham Hermit	48
The Gell Almshouses	53
Ickenham Green about the turn of the century	55
Ickenham Pond about the turn of the century	60
Ickenham Post Office 1911, with Miss Ellen Butler in the doorway	67
Orchard Cottage, site of the present library	71
Swakeleys Road on the occasion of the 1908 Marathon	74
Ickenham Pond: at left the 'Fox and Geese' and forge	77
The forge next to the 'Fox and Geese' about 1910	78
Ickenham Village showing Llewellyn Wood's Forge	79
Ladies plough team during the First World War	83
Panoramic view of Ickenham 1913	88-89
Map of Ickenham in 1983	90
Building on Swakeleys Road in the 1930's	91

ACKNOWLEDGEMENTS

I wish to thank everyone who helped prepare *The Story of Ickenham* for publication, but especially Carolynne Cotton, who compiled the index, Andrew Maxted, who designed the book, and Mary Pearce for her proof-reading and advice.

B.W.

INTRODUCTION

Morris Hughes was born in Ickenham in 1905, in the old shop-cum-post-office behind the Pump. (Number 4, the Cottages). He spent most of his life in the village. His great grandfather, Thomas Clavell Urry, and his great great grandfather were both tenants of Glebe Farm, which stood on the junction of Glebe and Clovelly Avenues. With such deep roots, it is not surprising that he was interested in Ickenham's history.

He witnessed many changes. In his life-time, the hamlet of three hundred people became a populous suburb of London He saw country lanes and horse-drawn transport replaced by a dual carriage-way and streams of cars. Some years ago, he decided to chronicle this transformation. His articles, published in various Middlesex journals, were expanded to make this book. Mr. Hughes wrote not as a detached historian but as a resident of long standing, who had a deep affection for Ickenham. His book blends history with reminiscences. The sketches of village scenes and characters as he remembered them are full of life and humour.

No great events have taken place in Ickenham, though famous men have sometimes visited the village. For hundreds of years, the rhythm of life in this small farming community barely altered. Therefore, the history that follows is not a chronological narrative. It focuses, instead, on certain topics and covers them from earliest to recent times.

I hope that this book may inspire some of its readers to take an active interest in their local heritage, whether they live in Ickenham or elsewhere. It is only through such interest that the past is preserved and places retain their character.

BRIAN WILLIAMS
Editor

Map

HAREFIELD

Dews Farm · Highway Farm · Springwell Green · Cook's Nest · Brick kiln · *RISELIP* · Riselip P...

Blackenbough · Brown's Wood · Crock · Riselip · Kings End · Riselip

Weston Lane · Ickenham · Field End · Riselip F...

Crab Tree Lane · Alderton Field · Mapit Field

Lea... Lane · Ryefield · Highfield · Grutedge Wood · Middle Field · Further Field · Bone Field · *RISELIP*

Golden Bridge · Grutedge Field

HERMINDS

Chapter One
Before 1066

Little is known about the early history of the area that became Ickenham. No traces of prehistoric man have been found in Ickenham itself. However, much evidence of his presence has been discovered in nearby areas and it is likely that Stone Age hunters ranged over Ickenham also.

The earliest finds belong to the Mesolithic period, about 8,000 to 4,000 B.C. At this time, human settlements were mostly along the banks of rivers such as the Thames, the Colne and the Lea. The rivers gave access to areas of dense forest, roamed by deer, wild cattle, elk and wild boar. With fire and wooden-handled flint axes, Mesolithic man cleared trees and undergrowth close to the water-side. His flint blades and scrapers have been found at Dewes Farm, south of Harefield.

During the Neolithic period (4,000 to 2,000 B.C.) settlers from the Continent gradually supplanted the Mesolithic inhabitants of Britain. The newcomers grew crops, herded cattle, made pottery and left behind them monuments of earth and stone. Six flint axes and an arrowhead from this era have been recovered at Harefield. The absence of pottery suggests that there was no permanent settlement.

The Iron Age, said to begin about 500 B.C., left a few traces in the locality. Iron Age pottery was discovered in a sand-pit and an iron spearhead was found on a hill overlooking the Colne. With the spearhead was a bone point exactly like one from an Iron Age burial at Grimthorpe, Yorkshire. It should be remembered that two notable centres of Iron Age culture existed not far away from Ickenham. There was a hill fort at modern Gerrard's Cross and a large temple on the site of Heathrow Airport.

In Ickenham there used to be evidence of an ancient earthwork, which may have dated from the Iron Age. It could be seen in the twelve acre field known as the Fir Walk. This field was in the angle formed by the eastern end of Swakeleys Drive and the curve of Long Lane towards Ickenham. An unnatural dip and rise of the ground ran parallel to Long Lane, about twenty or thirty yards from the hedge. At the northern edge of the field, where Long Lane bears slightly to the west, the road and earthwork merged. A continuation of the earthwork could be seen in Ickenham churchyard running parallel to the wall.

It is possible that this earthwork connected with the famous Grim's Dyke, still to be seen in Harrow. The Dyke would then have led from Stanmore Common to Bentley Priory, then through Grim's Dyke Golf Course, Hatch End, Pinner Green and Ruislip to Ickenham and possibly Uxbridge Common.

The purpose and age of Grim's Dyke have never been ascertained. The name is Anglo-Saxon; Grim was another name for Wodin or the Devil, who was often made responsible for mysterious phenomena in later ages. The Dyke

Facing: Ickenham area from John Rocque's map of Middlesex, 1754

itself, consisting of a mound sometimes accompanied by a ditch, is not Anglo-Saxon but much older, perhaps dating from 550 B.C. It may have been a tribal boundary or had some agricultural use.

At the time of the Roman invasion, in A.D. 43, the Ickenham area was a dense forest bordering the lands of a British tribe called the Catuvellauni. The most notable leaders of this tribe were Cunobelinus, who ruled 10-42 A.D., and his son, Caratacus, leader of the British resistance to Rome. The Catuvellauni would have hunted deer in the forest near Ickenham.

The best evidence of Roman occupation was found in the early 19th century by J. A. Partridge, then owner of Breakspear House, near Harefield. Whilst digging the foundations for a wall, he discovered "Roman sepulchres" along Drakes Hill. Unfortunately, no record of his finds has survived, apart from a brief reference in Redford and Riches' *History of Uxbridge* (1818). However, the discovery at Drakes Hill does lend credence to the theory that a Roman road passed near Harefield and Ickenham. This theory was stated in detail in *Roman roads in the South East*, a book produced by the Viatores group.

The conjectural road would have run from Verulamium (St. Albans) to Laleham via Watford, Batchworth Heath, Harefield, Uxbridge and West Drayton. The section of road nearest to Ickenham would be that following Harvil Road and passing the old Gospel Oak in Swakeleys Road on the way to Uxbridge Common. Such a route is difficult to trace because the area is built-up and much of it would have subsided, leaving only the agger or mound as a raised pathway. The Viatores claim to have followed sections of agger and also point to occasional discoveries of flint and pebbles as evidence of old road materials. Unfortunately, no more substantial evidence has ever come to light.

When the Romans left Britain in the 5th century A.D., the way was open for Germanic tribes to raid the coast and finally settle in this country. Place names bear witness to their invasion. At West Drayton (draeg-tun) the foreigners' ships were dragged ashore; a tribe called the Wixan settled at Uxbridge (Woxebruge); and a chieftain called Hildric gave his name to Hillingdon. As for Ickenham, it was the 'ham' or village of Ticca, another Anglo-Saxon leader.

The Domesday Book provides details of land ownership in Ickenham during the reign of Edward the Confessor (1042-1066). In this late Saxon period, there were three estates called 'Ticheham'. Two became the nucleus of the manor of Ickenham, whilst the third became part of Swakeleys manor.

Toki, a 'house carl' or bodyguard of King Edward, held two hides of land in "Ticheham". A hide was the land needed to support one household, and estimates of its size vary from sixty acres to twice that amount. Smaller tenants on this estate were Alwin, servant of Ulsi, with a hide and three virgates of land, and two sokemen, servants of Wulfheard, with two hides and one virgate. A 'virgate' was approximately thirty acres. 'Sokemen' held their land in return for certain specific services to their lord. Toki, Alwin and the two sokemen were all free to sell their land if they wished.

The second of the estates that became the manor of Ickenham was smaller and was held by two anonymous servants. Earl Leofwin's man held 2½ hides, whilst Ansgar the Constable's man held only one hide. The former could sell as he liked, the latter needed his lord's permission to do so.

The third estate was made up of two hides held by Aelmer, a servant of Wulfward Wight, who enjoyed freedom of sale. The manor of Swakeleys grew

Before 1066

from this small beginning to include much land outside the parish of Ickenham. By the 17th century, it comprised more than 2,000 acres.

For administrative purposes, Ickenham was included in the hundred of Elthorne. A hundred was a division of a county and consisted of ten tithings. The tithing was a group of ten freeholders living in a community and responsible to the King for the good conduct of each other. Middlesex, being densely wooded, could not support a large number of families, so there were only six hundreds. Each month, a hundred court would be held at some well-known land-mark. Elthorne Hundred, which took in most of the modern borough of Hillingdon, was named after a thorn tree growing on the land of a leader called "Aella". ("Aella's thorn"). The court was held under this tree.

No personal details of the lives of Toki, Alwin and the others have been recorded, but archaeological evidence from other parts of Anglo-Saxon England gives us a fair idea of their way of life. A farmer and his household would probably have lived in a long house with thatched roof and walls of wattle and daub. People and livestock were all under the same roof. Outbuildings, which were little more than pits with a tent-like thatch above, served as work-shops for weavers and potters.

The farm land would have consisted of three large fields divided into one acre strips. Such a strip, measuring 220×22 yards, was reckoned to be a day's ploughing with eight oxen. The crops would be wheat and barley or oats, and one field would always be left fallow for the year. There would also be meadows for cattle grazing and woodland where pigs rooted for mast. For the farmer and his household, life must have been a hard struggle with little leisure and no luxuries. They did enjoy considerable independence, but that was to change after 1066, when Ickenham came under the rule of Norman lords of the manor.

Chapter Two

Norman Lords and their Successors

As we all know, William of Normandy defeated the Anglo-Saxons at Hastings in 1066 and made himself ruler of England. He rewarded his followers by grants of conquered land and they became his tenants-in-chief, bound to fight for him if called upon to do so. The tenants-in-chief had tenants of their own, the lords of the manor, and beneath them were small tenant farmers. At the bottom of the social scale were the serfs.

In order to avoid disputes about the sums of money due to him from his tenants, the King ordered a national census. This "Description of England", as it was first called, would give an accurate summary of the extent, value and ownership of land in England. Eventually the "description" came to be known as Domesday Book for, just as each man had to give an account of himself to God on Judgement Day, so each Englishman had to give an account of himself to the King.

Commissioners were sent to the chief town of each county to take sworn evidence from barons, shire reeves and representatives of each hundred and village. The data was gathered at Winchester, where the King's clerks completed the summary in 1086. The three entries for "Ticheham", translated from the original Latin, are as follows:-

Ickenham 2 englishmen hold 3½ hides from Geoffrey,
Land for 2 ploughs; they are there.
3 villagers with ½ virgate each; 5 smallholders.
Meadow for 2 ploughs; pasture of the village livestock; woodland, 40 pigs.
Value of this land, 30s; when acquired the same; before 1066, 60s.

The Geoffrey referred to above was Geoffrey de Mandeville, a Norman who became a great landowner in England largely through the forfeited estates of Asgar the Constable, one of King Harold's men. His son, William de Mandeville, was Constable of the Tower of London. The most notorious of his descendants, also named Geoffrey, held sway over Middlesex, Hertfordshire, London and Essex during the Civil War between King Stephen and his queen, Matilda. He died, an outlaw and an excommunicate, in 1144. The second entry reads:

Manor Ickenham answers for 9½ hides. 3 men-at-arms and 1 Englishman hold it from Earl Roger. Land for 6 ploughs; 4 ploughs there; a further 2 possible. 6 villagers with 1 hide; 2 others with 1 hide and 1 virgate; 2 others with 2 virgates; 4 smallholders with 20 acres; 3 cottages. Meadow for 4 ploughs; pasture for the village livestock; woodland, 200 pigs. Total value £4; when acquired the same; before 1066 £6.

"Earl Roger" was Roger de Montgomery, Earl of Shrewsbury and

Norman Lords and their Successors

Arundel. He was a cousin of William the Conqueror, supplied sixty ships for the invasion fleet and commanded the right flank of the Norman force at the battle of Hastings. He died in 1093.

The nine and a half hides owned by de Montgomery formed the nucleus of the later Manor of Ickenham, which also included some of de Mandeville's land. The third entry in Domesday Book describes the area that would later form part of Swakeleys Manor:

> In ELTHORNE Hundred Robert Fafiton holds 2 hides in ICKENHAM from the King. Land for 1 plough, but it is not there now. Meadow for 1 plough; pasture for the village livestock; woodland, 30 pigs. Value of this land, 5s; when acquired 40s; before 1066, 40s.

There were four local manors, Ickenham, Tykenham, Swalcliff (Swakeleys), and Herses (Hercies). They extended in some cases into other parishes. The only one also known as a parish was Ickenham, and parts of the other three were within the parish. A lawsuit of 1453 adjudged that the manor of Tykenham was in the parish of Hillingdon. But this judgement probably referred only to the Manor House, as being the seat of the Lord of the Manor. Herses became part of the manor of Swalcliff while still being within the parish of Hillingdon.

The manor of Ickenham passed from Geoffrey de Mandeville to William de Brock, although some financial interest in the estate still rested with the de Mandeville family. An old document records that *"Eleanor, Duchess of Gloucester, heir to the Bohans and Mandevilles, died, seised of a fee in Ickenham, anno 1400"*. The word "seised" is constantly used in old documents, and means "having legal possession". From John, son and heir of William de Brock, it was conveyed to John Charlton, mercer and citizen of London, for life.

In 1348, the manor passed to Nicholas Shorediche, his wife and their heirs. The Shorediche family had been dispossessed of the manors of Hackney and Shoreditch at the time of the Norman Conquest. In the 14th century, a member of the family married a direct descendant of Geoffrey de Mandeville, uniting the two manorial families. The manor remained in Shorediche hands for many generations.

The Lord of the Manor in 1819 was George Robinson. In 1853, it was jointly held by Francis Robinson and Henry Hewitt Mason. Three years later, the rights were in the hands of three men, Henry Hewitt Mason, William Bird and Samuel Strong.

The advowson of St. Giles, the parish church of Ickenham, was in the hands of the Shorediche family. One member, John Shorediche, was rector from 1714 until 1725. Thomas Clarke of Spring Gardens in the City of Westminster acquired the advowson from the trustees of Robert Shorediche in 1743. Thereafter, the descendants of Thomas Clarke were to play no small part in the life and destiny of Ickenham. After the death of Thomas, his son, the Rev. Thomas Clarke, was appointed rector of the parish on the 7th of April, 1747. The year after his induction he married Mary, the daughter of Thomas Blencowe of the Manor of Hercies in the parish of Hillingdon. In 1750, he bought the Swakeleys mansion and manor.

His wife died in 1771, at the age of 44 years, and was buried in the village churchyard. The inscription on her memorial tablet on the west wall of the church is a glowing tribute from her grieving husband. The Manor of Hercies

13

The Story of Ickenham

became the property of the Rev. Clarke by will. It was thereafter added to, and included in, the Manor of Swakeleys. The Hercies Manor House then became known as Hercies Farm and was occupied by members of the Clarke family. It was demolished about the middle of the 20th century to make way for a housing estate.

When he had recovered from the shock of the death of his first wife, the Rev. Clarke married Frances, the daughter of Thomas Truesdale of Harefield Place, by whom he had three sons. At his death in 1796, he was succeeded by his eldest son, Thomas Truesdale Clarke.

It was this Thomas Truesdale Clarke (1774-1840) who in 1813 built a bridge over the River Pinn in Back Lane (Swakeleys Road) and promoted the Church of England School in Ickenham. He was a local magnate and his mysterious death caused a sensation. He was found drowned in a shallow brook in the parish of Hillingdon. Suicide was suspected but not proved. Whilst the inquest was in progress, James Winch, a stud groom employed by Mrs. Clarke's brother, hanged himself.

The second Thomas Truesdale Clarke (1802-1890) was also an important local figure. He was Deputy Lieutenant of Elthorne Hundred, Magistrate for Uxbridge Division, a Commissioner of property and income tax and a trustee of Uxbridge savings bank. He became Lord of the manor of Ickenham in 1865 and chose to hold his courts baron in "The Coach and Horses", instead of at the manor house. To the villagers, he was always "Squire Clarke".

When he died in 1890, he was succeeded by his son, William Capel

Home Farm about 1900

Norman Lords and their Successors

Manor Farm, 1960

Clarke. He married Clara, the daughter and co-heiress of Thomas Thornhill of Fixby Hall in Yorkshire. He added his wife's name to his own. Their joint coat-of-arms may be seen on their memorial tablet on a wall in the parish church.

The next holder of the manor was Randolph Clarke-Thornhill, who was in turn succeeded by his brother, Thomas Bryan Clarke-Thornhill. After a close association with the affairs of Ickenham, which had prevailed for a hundred and eighty years, the influence of the Clarke family came to an end in 1923. At the direction of Thomas Bryan Clarke-Thornhill, who was then living at his other home at Rushton Hall in Northamptonshire, the Ickenham manor was sold. He ordered that it should be broken into small lots in order that the tenants should be able to buy the property in which they lived. This regard for the tenants was not something new, for during the First World War years, any tenant serving in the forces was excused the payment of his rent.

Most of the farmers bought the farms which they occupied, and a number of the cottage tenants bought their homes. Hercies Farm, Ivy House Farm and Milton Farm live on in the names of roads. Before being demolished to make way for houses they, together with other properties, continued to be used as farms. Long Lane Farm, Copthall Farm and Home Farm are still in use as farms.

At the break-up of the estate, Manor Farm, once Ickenham manor house, returned to a member of the Shorediche family. The present building is

15

mainly 15th century work. It was built on the site of an ancient "Motte-tower", a fortress-like building largely constructed of flint. Surrounding it was a wide and deep moat, filled with inky-black, seemingly bottomless water. Parts of this defence may still be seen.

Some parts of the house were demolished in the 19th century, when Thomas Truesdale Clarke became Lord of the Manor of Ickenham with Swakeleys as his seat. A 17th century staircase was preserved, together with some other interesting parts of the building. Thereafter, the house and adjoining land were let as Manor Farm to a tenant farmer. The house is approached by a narrow winding lane from the east side of Long Lane close by Douay Martyrs Roman Catholic School. This lane also services Long Lane Farm.

Chapter Three

Swakeleys: The Manor and the House

The earliest reference to a name like Swakeleys was in 1326. It was recorded that Robert de Swalclyve and his wife, Joan, and son, William, owned premises in "Herefield, Tykenham and Ickenham next Woxebrugges." The name "de Swalclyve" is linked with the Oxfordshire village of Swalcliff, pronounced "Swaycliff", from which is derived Swakeleys.

The de Swalclyves had dealings with Roger Rikeman, also known as Lapin, a money-lender. They acquired some local property from him in 1329, and disposed of some of it, four years later, to William de Gauger and his wife, Sarah.

Robert de Swalclyve must be the "Robert de Wykeham, lord of Swalcleve", who in 1347 owed £40 to Roger Rikeman, the sum "to be levied in default of payment on his lands and chattles in co. Oxon." Wickham Park, like Swalcliff, was in Oxfordshire, near Banbury. Apparently, Robert de Swalclyve did not manage to salvage his financial affairs. In 1350, Boniface Lapyn released to John de Charlton all right to those lands in Ickenham which had been in the ownership of Robert de Swalclyve and his wife, Joan.

Sir Thomas de Charlton died in 1410 leaving no children. His sister, Anne, married William Knightley, by whom she had a son named Thomas. He inherited all his uncle's property and took his uncle's name as his own and was later knighted. This Sir Thomas de Charlton married Elizabeth, the daughter of Sir Adam Frauceys, who had been knighted for his services in the Wat Tyler rebellion.

Sir Thomas died in 1448 and was succeeded by his son, yet another Sir Thomas. He became the Member of Parliament for Middlesex and later was made the Speaker of the House of Commons in 1453. After his death in 1465, in his Inquisitio Post Mortem, it was stated that he was "seised of the Manors of Covelhall (Cowley), Swalclyve, hercyes and Litilhelyndon", which he had put in the hands of trustees for the purposes of his will. The manors of Swalclyve and the two in the parishes of Hillyngdon and Ikenham were said to be held by Richard Willy and his wife, in the wife's right as of her "manor of Ikenham".

At the time of Sir Thomas's death, his son, Sir Richard, was 15 years of age. He died twenty years later at the Battle of Bosworth. His name was included in the Act of Attainder passed when Henry VII came to the throne. Sir Richard's wife, Elizabeth, was not dispossessed of the manors of Swalcliffe and Covelhall. The crown granted their reversion, with Sir Richard's other properties, to Sir Thomas Bourchier and his wife, who was the sister of Sir Richard.

Sir Thomas Bourchier died, and one of his executors, Sir John Peeche, obtained a grant of reversion of Swakeleys in 1510, but he died without heirs. Eleven years later, the reversion was granted to Sir Henry Courtenay, Earl of Devon. In 1531, he obtained a licence to alienate Swalcliffe to Sir William Fitzwilliam as trustee for Ralph Pexall and his wife. In his will, Ralph Pexall calls himself "of Swalcliff in Middlesex and Beaureper, Co. of Hampshire". He also

17

Swakeleys from an engraving of 1800

draws attention to his "Mansion house in Fleet Street" in the suburbs of London.

His son, Sir Richard Pexall, was twice married. His first wife was Lady Eleanor Paulet, daughter of the Marquess of Winchester. They had four daughters. His second wife was also named Eleanor. She was the daughter of John Cotgrave of Chester. Sir Richard styled himself as of "Beaureper, Steventon Manor, Fleet Street London and Swarcliffe Manor in Middlesex, Knight."

His daughters all married, Anne to Bernard Brocas of Horton, Margery to Oliver Beckett and later to Francis Cotton. Elizabeth, sometimes called Ellen, was married to John Hobson, and Barbara to Anthony Brydges.

Margery had an heir by Oliver Beckett. During her father's lifetime, she lived at Swakeleys with her second husband by whom she had a daughter. In the St. Giles parish register appears the following, under the entry dated 1554: "*Barbara, the dowghter of John Cawghton* (this is obviously a mistake and refers to Francis Cotton) *of Swakeleys Place and Margery hys wyfe, was chrystenyde the muday* (Monday) *before our Ladyday thassupcon* (The Assumption) *beying the 13 day off Auguste. The godfather Mr. Say, the godmothers Barbara the wife of Mr. Brydges and Helyn the wyf of Mr. Edmude Shoredyche.*"

Anne and Bernard Brocas lived at Swakeleys from 1575 until the death of Bernard in 1589. Their son, Pexall, was knighted in 1603. He was married to Margaret, the daughter of Thomas Shirley of Wiston in Sussex. He seems to have been in financial difficulties. From a fine of 1591 his wife's father took over "ten parts of the manor of Swaclyff alias Swakeley" from his daughter and her husband. The remainder of the estate was still in the hands of Sir Richard Pexall's daughters. Sir Thomas Shirley was in possession in 1593, but a few years later he sold the "manor of Swacklies" to Robert Bromley. This was made known when Richard Walter of the Middle Temple brought proceedings in Chancery.

Richard Walter complained that Michael Shorediche, the Lord of Ickenham Manor, had four years previously distrained certain cattle which belonged to the complainant being in "Swacklies Parke" for twenty-four shillings for quit rent. Richard Walter held at that time "Swacklies Parke" from Sir Thomas Shirley "then lord and donor of the manor of Swacklies of which the park was parcel". Shorediche had promised that he would show Sir Thomas and Mr. Altam of Gray's Inn, being "Of counsel" with Sir Thomas, proof that the rent was due.

The evidence showed that the charge should be shared with Jn. Stamborowes of Hercies and Jn. Nicholas who held other parcels of the manor. Shorediche had promised to collect it, but had failed in the undertaking. Robert Bromley had since purchased the manor of "Swacklies" from Sir Thomas Shirley. In his answer, Michael Shorediche said the distress warrant was taken out in April "of the thirty-fourth year of the reign of Queen Elizabeth of England" (1592). He submitted that the reversion of Swakeleys Park was not in Sir Thomas Shirley but in Pexall Brocas. He did not know if there was indeed a manor of Swakeleys or not.

He went to Sir Thomas because, soon after the distress, he was the buyer of the land. Michael Shorediche produced a deed made by Sir Richard Pexall in which he had agreed to pay the ancestor of Michael, namely, Robert Shorediche, twelve shillings and three pence quit rent about the year 1554.

Robert Bromley sold Swakeleys to John Bingley in 1606. Bromley, an "Officer of the Court of Exchequer", filed a complaint against his tenant, one William Cragg, an "Attorney of the Court of Common Pleas", in 1616. Cragg's tenancy was subject to the owner of the property and his stewards holding court for the manor of "Swackliffe" or "Swackley".

There is a document which records that Henrietta Bencraft, who owned land in the locality, would, at the next General Court Baron for the Manor of Swakeley, surrender into the hands of the Lord of the said Manor a stable, part of a barn and some pasture land near Little Hillingdon Field in the same Manor.

John Bingley was knighted in 1618. Eleven years later, he sold Swakeleys to Edmund Wright, an alderman of the City of London. During the same year, the new owner was elected to the office of Sheriff of the City of London. He built the present house in 1638. His initials E.W., and the date appear in several places high on the building, including the leaden rain-water heads. He was made Lord Mayor of London for the year 1640-41, following the removal by Act of Parliament of Sir William Acton. Sir Edmund's will, made in 1641, was proved on August 22nd, 1643. In it the Manor of Swakeleys was settled on his daughter, Margaret, but was later assigned to his daughter Katherine, the wife of Sir James Harington, "subject to inviting the rest of the family to Swakeleys once a year for Fourteen days".

Sir James Harington was one of those who sat in judgement at the trial of King Charles I. At the restoration of the Monarchy, he avoided the fate of his fellow Cromwellian conspirators by escaping to France in 1660.

Robert Vyner bought Swakeleys House and Manor from the wife of Sir James, who had remained at the house after her husband had fled to France. Robert Vyner was knighted in 1665 and was made a baronet the following year. He was a Sheriff of the City of London, a goldsmith, and friend of Charles II.

The Story of Ickenham

When his London house was destroyed in the Great Fire of London in 1666, he was given Royal permission to store his great wealth of gold, jewels and plate in the strong rooms of Windsor Castle.

When Sir Robert Vyner was made Lord Mayor of London in 1674, King Charles II attended the mayoral banquet at the Guildhall. Here is the account of that banquet, written for *The Spectator* by Sir Richard Steele:

"*Charles II more than once dined with his good citizens of London on their lord-mayor's day, and did so the year that Sir Robert Vyner was mayor. Sir Robert was a very loyal man, and, if you will allow the expression, very fond of his sovereign; but, what with the joy he felt in his heart for the honour done him by his prince, and through the warmth he was in with the continual toasting healths to the royal family, his lordship grew a little fond of his majesty, and entered into a familiarity not altogether so graceful in so public a place. The King understood very well how to extricate himself in all kinds of difficulties, and with a hint to the company to avoid ceremony, stole off and made towards his coach, which stood ready for him in the Guildhall yard. But the mayor liked his company so well, and was grown so intimate, that he pursued him hastily, and catching him fast by the hand, cried out with a vehement oath, and accent, 'Sir, you shall stay and take t'other bottle.' The airy monarch looked kindly at him over his shoulder, and with a smile and graceful air (for I saw him and do know), repeated the line of the old song: "He that's drunk is as great as a king," and immediately returned back and complied with his landlord.*"

Another who wrote in quite a different vein was the diarist and Admiralty civil servant, Samuel Pepys. In his diary under the date 7th of September, 1665, appears the following entry: "*To Branford...*(Brentford) *...there a coach of Mr. Povey's stood ready for me, and he at his house ready to come in, and so we together merrily to Swakeleys, Sir R. Viner's. He took us up and down with great respect, and showed us all his house and grounds: and it is a place not very moderne in the garden nor house, but the most uniforme in all that ever I saw; and some things to excess. Pretty to see over the screen of the hall (put up by Sir J. Harington, a Long Parliament man) the King's head, and My Lord of Essex on one side, and Fairfax on the other; and upon the other side of the screene the parson of the parish and the lord of the manor and his sisters. The window-cases, door-cases, and chimneys of all the house are marble. He showed me a black boy that he had that had died of a consumption, and being dead, he caused him to be dried in an oven, and lies there entire in a box.*"

It was generally supposed by servants that the mummified body of the black boy had been put into a cupboard which was situated halfway up the servants' or backstairs. The door had been sealed and no one bothered or dared to open it, thus giving point to the legend which had been handed down from old servants to newcomers through the years. When the house became empty, the family of Arthur N. Gilbey having left before the sale in 1923, workmen of the estate builder unsealed the cupboard. It was empty. There was no box, no body nor anything else inside. Pepys continues: "*By and by to dinner, where his lady I find yet handsome, but hath been a very handsome woman; now is old. Hath brought him near £100,000 and now he lives, no man in England in greater plenty, and commands both King and Council with his credit he gives them. After dinner Sir Robert led us up to his long gallery, very fine, above stairs; and better, or such, furniture I never did see. After all this and ending the chief business to my content about getting a promise of some money of him, we took leave, being exceeding well*

Swakeleys: The Manor and the House

Swakeleys 1819

treated here, and a most pleasant journey we had back."

Samuel Pepys visited Swakeleys again the same year with the same object in view, the borrowing of money. It was on Sunday the 15th of October, when he met Sir Robert Vyner: *"He was coming just from church, and we went, he and I into his garden to discourse of money, but none is to be had."*

Sir Robert was the Lord Mayor of London for the year 1674-75. He died in 1688 leaving no children, but three brothers. One of them, Thomas, was Dean of Gloucester and Prebendary of Windsor. He had a son named Thomas who died in Rome while on a visit. He had expressed the wish before going that he should be interred in Ickenham. His body was therefore brought back for immurement in the Swakeleys Vault in St. Giles' church.

His only child Robert represented Lincoln in the House of Commons for many years. He died in 1777 at the age of ninety-four, but long before his death he had sold Swakeleys to Benjamin Lethieullier. At Benjamin's death it passed by his will to the Rev. Lascelles Iremonger.

In 1743, the entire estate and the manors of Swakeleys and Ickenham passed by deed of sale to the Clarke family. Randolph Clarke-Thornhill, grandson of The Squire, was the last of the family to live there. The house and estate were let to Mr. Arthur N. Gilbey at the end of the 19th century. He was a brother of Sir Walter Gilbey, and his partner in the wine and spirit business which bears their names. He was an ardent lover of horses. The well-appointed stables and coach houses were put to good use. They formed two sides of the kitchen courtyard. Above the stables were the granaries and over the coach houses good living quarters for the ostlers.

Mr. Gilbey driving his four-in-hand was a familiar sight along the local roads, particularly when he was on his way to or from the Great Western Station at the north end of Ickenham. The First World War brought this to an end. The War Department commandeered all the good horses and most of the

The Story of Ickenham

haystacks for use by the cavalry. A car took the place of the carriage, and the coachman became a chauffeur.

Mr. Gilbey was also an enthusiastic and proficient player of the ancient game of croquet. Many famous people have played on the croquet lawns at Swakeleys. Soon after the family took up residence, the Croquet Championship for All England was held here. Mr. Gilbey gave a trophy to be competed for annually by private houses. It was known as the Arthur Gilbey Cup. When the manor was put on the market, the Gilbey family moved to Maidenhead where they had bought an estate.

The mansion and the land, including the park and woodlands which formed the main lot in the sale, was bought by estate agents for intended housing development. To save the mansion from demolition, it was bought by Humphrey John Talbot, a near kinsman of the Earl of Shrewsbury. He was anxious that the fine old house with its outbuildings and attractive and well-watered parkland should be preserved. With the help of the Society for the Preservation of Ancient

Swakeleys – a modern view

Swakeleys: The Manor and the House

Buildings, he formulated a plan with this object in view. Eventually the Sports Association of the Foreign Office bought Swakeleys for use as their headquarters and sports ground. A condition of sale was that Humphrey Talbot retained possession of the first floor as tenant of the Sports Association.

During his residence there he gave a coming-out ball for one of his nieces, the daughter of his deceased brother. One of the many well-known people he entertained at Swakeleys was Queen Mary, wife of George V.

Humphrey Talbot owned a remarkable collection of clocks, gathered on his travels round the world. One from the Far East was made entirely from jarrah, known in the trade as iron-wood. Another from China was operated by the dripping of water on to a wheel. He took these clocks, as well as some beautiful tapestries, when he moved to France shortly before the Second World War. The author had the pleasure of packing the collection. When France was over-run by the Nazis, the whole collection was lost. Humphrey Talbot managed to escape to England, where he died soon afterwards.

During the Second World War, Swakeleys was used by the Army. It then stood empty for some years. In 1955 it was sold to the London Postal Region Sports Club. Since 1982 the house has belonged to Swakeleys House Ltd., a company formed by three residents of The Avenue, Ickenham. They hope to restore the house and make its grounds more accessible to the public. To finance the restoration, offices will be built and leased at the rear of the house.

THE HOUSE

No physical traces remain of the old manor house replaced by the present Swakeleys. However, some information about its size and appearance can be gleaned from the abstract of Exchequer Proceedings for 1616, in the case of John Bingley versus William Cragg. The abstract was printed in Walter Godfrey's *Swakeleys, Ickenham* (13th monograph of the London Survey Committee, 1933).

The legal case mentioned above revolved around certain alterations made on the grounds of the old manor house by Bingley, the owner. It is clear that the old manor house had a moat, which Bingley filled in, or so he claimed, because the water was "corrupt and unhealthful". He then built a brick wall around the estate as a new defence.

There was also a large orchard in the grounds. Bingley dug up 100 trees "of warden's pears, apples of divers sorts, plums, cherries etc" but claimed he had replaced them with "at least 300 new fruit trees". The tenant, Cragg, complained that Bingley had also spoiled the dove house and driven away all but "three pair" of the "120 pair" of pigeons which once roosted there.

Other damage alleged by Cragg included the digging-up of the hop plot and the felling of so much timber that firewood now had to be bought. Five of the six acres of pasture for "horses, kine and other cattle" were also supposed to have been torn up by workmen's horses and carts. Another four acres had been spoiled by Bingley's manufacturing; he had made 800,000 bricks in the grounds.

From such references, there emerges the picture of a sizeable, thriving and almost self-sufficient estate. Information about the house is less precise but apparently it included a "Great Chamber", called "The King's Chamber", as well as a hall, "a great parlour", a kitchen and a buttery. One of the larger rooms would have been used for sessions of the manorial court.

While on the subject of vanished houses connected with the manor, some mention should be made of "Pynchester". In 1966-67, local archaeologists

23

40074. SWAKELEYS, ICKENHAM, NEAR UXBRIDGE.

excavated the remains of a house on a moated site a few hundred yards north of the footbridge in Copthall Road, Ickenham. They hoped to find traces of "Pynchester", which was, according to Lysons' *Parishes in the county of Middlesex not in the Environs of London* (1800) the home of the noble family of Hastings in the early 16th century. Amongst other items, the excavations revealed a 14th century hearth measuring 11 feet square, an Edward III silver penny and a large quantity of a type of pottery known as Surrey ware.

On the edge of modern Ickenham, on the west side of Breakspear Road, can be seen the moat of the old Brackenbury manor house. The manor was named after Thomas Brackenbury, a London merchant who received a grant of land from the lord of Harefield in 1355. By 1558 the manor was included in Harefield. The present house dates from the 17th century and was once used by the Newdigates of Harefield.

Returning to Swakeleys, the surviving house of that name was built by Sir Edmund Wright between 1629 and 1638. This brick mansion replaced the earlier house which was, presumably, a timber-framed structure with wattle in-filling, like Ickenham Manor. The inventory of Sir Thomas Charlton's goods, made after his death in 1465, refers to a house, probably Swakeleys manor, with 19 rooms, a chapel, stables and outbuildings. It must have been an impressive house, but by Sir Edmund Wright's time it would have seemed old fashioned and incommodious.

Swakeleys about 1910

      In his book *Greater London*, published in 1893, Edward Walford said that, after Holland House, Swakeleys was "the most interesting Jacobean house in the whole county of Middlesex. The gardens are quaint and trim, laid out in something of the old-fashioned style and a long avenue of elms adorns the front of the house to the south." This lovely avenue was destroyed by Dutch Elm disease in the late 1960s.

      The house is built with a central part and four projecting wings. Two are on the west carriage front, and two on the garden front on the eastern side of the building. The ground plan is rather in the shape of the letter H.

      Passing through the main door from the carriage front into the hall, the well-appointed gun-room is on the left. The Hall to the right is large and paved with great flag-stones. At each intersection are small black marble tiles. In a large central square, the pattern is set diagonally to contrast with the wide surround.

      Much has been written about the screen erected by Sir James Harington. It is an imposing work, standing across the northern end of the Hall to form a kind of passage from the entrance towards the stairs and garden door. It was constructed about 1655 and is probably the work of John Colt, junr., nephew of Maximilian Colt. Young John was a carver who later became assistant to Le Sueur. The main structure of the screen is wood with well-executed embellishments in plaster. It is painted to give the effect of stone and marble. There are three arches, the central one having a greater span than the others. A pair of lions crouch on the pediment of the central arch, and face the bust of King Charles I. Below them are the heads of two cherubs.

The side arches each have a shield of arms, each shield being held by a pair of cherubs. The bust of the King is flanked on one side by that of the Baron Fairfax, and on the other by the space where the bust of the Earl of Essex once stood. This bust is now in the parish church of St. Giles. Other works which adorned the screen were sculptures of the rector of the parish, the Lord of the Manor and his sisters. It is well that Samuel Pepys kept a diary or this might not have been known, for some of these have disappeared. It may be that the screen was built to provide a proper setting for the bust of the King, which was already in Sir James Harington's possession. There is little doubt that the bust is the work of Peter Bennier, who was sculptor to Charles I.

The massive marble fireplace near to the screen carries a bust of Ben Jonson in the centre of the shelf, with Milton and Harington, one on each side. The wrought-iron fire-back bears a war-like scene and the initials N.L., and the date ANNO 1695.

The fine oaken staircase is remarkable for the paintings which decorate the walls and ceiling. They are thought to be the work of Robert Streater, (1624-1680), but the late Edward Croft-Murray doubted this attribution. The Death of Dido is depicted on the south wall. The Queen, a wound in her side, is supported by another woman. In the foreground are two amorine holding a lighted torch.

On the north wall is The Founding of the City of Lavinium. Aeneas stands in Roman costume, wearing a helmet. A turbaned figure stands before other men, one of whom holds the plans of the City, which can be seen in the background.

The painting on the west wall is a landscape with a bridge. Seated on a pedestal and holding a bow is a small boy. The ceiling is painted to represent the sky. Juno is seated on a rainbow on which lean three amorine, one of them holding a peacock. Iris is seated on the clouds.

The panelling with which the Dining Room walls are completely covered is probably older than the house itself. When Sir Edmund Wright built the present house, he was so impressed with the quality of the craftsmanship in the old house that he used much of it in the construction of the new building. Another room in the north-east wing, with its door at the head of the stairs, was beautifully and completely panelled. This panelling, too, was most likely older than the house. When the estate was broken up, the panelling in this room was all removed.

The Great Chamber has been variously called the Ball Room and the Long Gallery. It is a magnificent room on the first floor, forty-two feet long and twenty-three feet wide. The boards of the original floor run from one end of the room to the other in one length. They are of pinewood, eighteen inches wide at one end and three inches at the other. Laid alternately, wide end to narrow end, each of the boards covers twenty-one inches. Owing to the wear this floor has suffered through the years, a new one has been laid over it.

An alcove, one step above this floor level, occupies the space above the ground floor front entrance loggia. This is the minstrel gallery where music was once played. The alcove ceiling has a central wreath with a cherub blowing at each corner.

The ceiling of the Great Chamber is sixteen feet high and is divided

The Great Chamber, Swakeleys

into fifteen panels. The plaster mouldings have laurel wreaths with cherubs' heads looking down at each corner. Magnificent 17th century panelling covers the walls, and on the side opposite to the alcove are two fine grey marble fire-places.

The outside walls of the house bear evidence of the date when the mansion was rebuilt. Several rain-water heads have the date 1638 embossed on them. Others have the initials of Sir Edmund Wright, E.W. One, much larger than the rest, high above the kitchen courtyard, has both date and initials. All have been well cast in lead. The workmanship cannot be fully appreciated from the ground.

Beyond the carriage front is an extensive lawn ending at a large lake with two well-wooded islands. There are three carriage drives leading to the house. The one most in use leads from Back Lane, now Swakeleys Road. At the entrance to this drive were two cottages and a large pair of ornate iron gates hung on massive brick piers. The cottages were the homes of workers. They have been converted into one private residence. The drive, now known as The Avenue, passed through the woodland called Home Cover. In a clearing to the left were two more cottages, one the home of the head gamekeeper, the other the home of the butler of Swakeleys. Each cottage had a back gate opening on to the village cricket field (Ivy House Road is here now), from which a footpath led to the courtyard and kitchen entrance of the mansion.

Leaving the woodlands, the drive passed alongside a field known as

The Story of Ickenham

Dovehouse Meadow, so called because of the dovehouse which stood at the end in a small covert named Park Clump. This dovehouse was a 17th century building of red brick, with a pyramid roof of red tiles, surmounted by a timber lantern. The tiles, and probably the bricks, were made at a spot in the north of the estate known still as The Tile Kilns. The building was about twenty feet square, and there were small oval openings in the sides which gave the birds access to the lofts. The lower part of the building was an ice-house.

Contrary to a published story, this was not damaged by Hitler's bombs. It was damaged by local vandals to such an extent that not a tile was left on the roof, and the rest was badly defaced. In the interest of safety the building was demolished, after giving pleasure for more than two hundred years.

Just beyond the Dovehouse the drive forked, the road on the left into the courtyard and farm buildings, the one on the right to the carriage door of the house. It then passed on south through the avenue of elms to turn left along the end of Firwalk field. It then emerged into Long Lane by Cruickshank's Lodge after passing through Long Lane Cover. The gates here were similar to those at the Swakeleys Road entrance. This lodge was the home of the head gardener, and it was named after him.

The West Lodge, which was demolished many years ago, stood opposite to the South Lodge of the Harefield Place estate. At the entrance of this drive was a heavy timber gate hung on massive posts, all products of the estate timber yard. Close by this lodge was the estate gravel pit and a large pond well-stocked with fish. This drive ran from the West Lodge through the Common Plantation to emerge between the open fields of Swakeleys Farm. A small hump-backed bridge carried it over the River Pinn, and on through The Clump and Bullock House Cover. The road still runs along the west side of the lake, to turn at the north end and join up with the other drive by the dovehouse. There were many footpaths which took one across various parts of the estate, from one farm to another, through meadows and woods. Many of these have been diverted in the interests of expediency, or incorporated in new roads.

Chapter Four
The Churches

The parish church of St. Giles was built largely in the early part of the 14th century. It is of flint and red brick, with a roof of red sand-faced tiles made at the nearby kilns. It replaced an ancient wooden structure of a much earlier period. In the parish register, the date of the first recorded rector is given as 1335.

The nave is the earliest part of the present building. This was used for worship while the chancel was under construction. Evidence of this may be seen by the piscina built into the south wall behind the pulpit, for use with a temporary altar. Before the building of the north aisle by William Say in 1575, the vestry was in the roof above the nave. It was reached by a staircase on the north wall. Evidence of this was revealed when the fabric of the church was being restored in 1921-22. Rows of nails and pieces of moulding, and crudely painted designs, indicated the size of a small upper room.

Above the nave and chancel was a whitewashed plaster ceiling. The architect, the late Mr. W. A. Forsyth, had the ceiling removed to expose the beams, braces and rafters of a fine oaken king-post roof. The previously exposed beams had been painted with successive coats of a dark red paint. The paint was removed to reveal the distinctive roof timbers in the natural beauty of the wood. The rafters, collars and king-post trusses are now completely uncovered, with the plaster work between the rafters. Mr. W. A. Forsyth was the consulting architect to Salisbury Cathedral, Rochester Cathedral and St. Margaret's, Westminster, among others.

When the north aisle had been completed, and the upper room and staircase removed, an organ, which probably superseded the flute, harp, sackbut and other kinds of music, was placed several feet from this new north wall at the eastern end. This space, with a curtain to screen it from the congregation, was the new vestry.

At the north-west corner of the church was the Swakeleys Vault, built in the 17th century by Sir James Harington. On three sides were deep upright niches built to accommodate coffins standing on end. More coffins were laid on the floor, and yet more coffins laid upon them. One small coffin is still immured in the wall, and several remain beneath the floor. All had heavy lead linings and were long, broad and deep. Before each immurement, access was gained by taking down the built-up entrance, there being no door. After the committal, the opening was bricked up again.

Early in 1914, a faculty was obtained whereby the coffins could be removed to a large grave in the north-west corner of the churchyard. They went to this new resting place on rollers travelling on stout timbers, so great was their weight. When all had been removed, the opening was sealed for the last time. The World War prevented the proposed work of converting the vacant vault into a vestry. After the war, work went ahead and a doorway was cut, giving access to the church. During the 1921-22 restoration, the vault was converted into a vestry.

The Story of Ickenham

*The Font,
St. Giles' Church*

The oak door was made of timber grown on the estate. Where the organ and vestry had been, choir stalls were built, facing south towards the chancel. The organ was re-sited beneath the belfry. After two further removals, the organ pipes are now actually in the belfry, with the console at the north end of the church.

The font, an exquisitely carved piece of work, stands beneath the belfry. It was returned to the church after doing service at Swakeleys as a tea caddy for many years. It was handed back to the church by Miss Helen Cochrane, cousin of Thomas Bryan Clarke-Thornhill, the last Lord of the Manor of Ickenham. It was he who gave the gilded weather vane to the church. It was mounted during the restoration and superseded an inconspicuous arrow. Doubtless it was overlooked that whereas the golden cock has no significance, the arrow is a part of the insignia of St. Giles. The cock had served for many years on the stables and coach houses at Swakeleys.

The belfry and spire are supported by four upright beams of oak, curved braces and moulded joists. There are four bells. The smallest is a sanctus bell dated 1582. It was probably the only one when the spire was a small, tiled pyramid roof with open sides. Of the others, one was known to the villagers as

The Churches

"the death bell". It was tolled at the death of a villager and again at the funeral. The code used at the beginning of the tolling indicated the age of the dead person: three rings for the young, two threes for the middle aged and three threes for the old. Each code was followed by the slow tolling at thirty second intervals for half an hour.

Another was known as "the ten o'clock bell". No service was held at that time, but this bell was rung sharply to let everyone know that in one short hour the morning service was due to begin. In another chapter, it will be seen that failure to attend church at least once each Sunday was a punishable offence. It may be that the bell was rung at ten o'clock in order to save folk from unwittingly committing this offence. Custom dies hard in rural districts, and this one continued until the 1920s. Immediately the morning service was over, this same bell would again be rung sharply for a few moments. This was to let the staff at Swakeleys know that the family were on their way back home for lunch.

The largest bell bears the inscription "Sancte Necolae ora Pro Nobis", and was cast in 1510. Another was cast in 1589. Two of the bells have coins let into them, probably for dating purposes. These coins are in such a position that it is impossible to read them, except by the use of a mirror, as a beam is quite close. The elm bell wheels were extensively repaired during the church restoration for which the Rev. Hugh Bannister Langton made himself responsible. He and his wife started the restoration fund by donating fifty pounds each.

Before the organ was installed beneath the belfry, the space was open to the nave and the bell ropes hung straight down through the timbered ceiling. It was not possible to ring the bells in the usual way; they were merely swung from side to side. By this means, the sexton, James Gladdy, was able to ring one with each hand. He had been known to ring the third one with his foot on festive and other special occasions.

The big bells were stopped when the organ voluntary began. The last few moments before the service commenced were indicated by a short period of ringing on the Sanctus bell. This one has been known for many generations as "The Tinker" or "Ting-Tang". When the organ was installed beneath the belfry, the bells were fixed, and by a system of ropes running on pulley wheels, the tongues were made to hit the bells.

A story is told about the time when the bell wheels were being repaired. It seems that the three workmen lost track of time until one of them felt the pangs of hunger. The one with the watch told his hungry mate that they should have knocked-off work a couple of hours earlier. So they blew out the candles, which were the only source of light, and descended the upright Jacob's ladder to find the church in darkness. The sexton had long since returned from his work as a wood-cutter, locked the church and gone to his home. The lock was a massive affair which could not be forced and the windows were either stained glass or had iron bars built into the masonry. The three prisoners clambered up the ladder and, each taking a hammer, rang the bells as they have never been rung before, or since. This brought the old sexton at the double and is perhaps the real origin of the saying, "Hell's bells!"

In common with most old churches, St. Giles' is rich in memorial tablets. One of the earliest is a fine brass at the south side of the east window to the memory of William Say, with effigies of himself, his wife Isobell, and their sixteen children, which reads: *"William Say, gentleman of Ickenham, Register of Her Majestie in Cawses Ecclesiasticall, and Procter of the Arches."*

The Story of Ickenham

He was the builder of the north aisle. He was not fully paid for this work, for in his will, dated the 4th of March, 1581, he draws the attention of Sir Henry Kendall, Parson of Ickenham, to the fact that the parishioners are in his debt for bricks for the new aisle, but that he will be content to have "the pewes for himself and his house". He bequeathed ten loads of gravel for mending "The Highwaie foote bridge". (Ickenham bridge, which had already been built by him). He mentions his sons, Robert, married, Thomas William, "nowe Mr. Chancellor of Winchester", Edward and John. Also named are his sons-in-law, Thomas Haydon, Mr. Shorediche, Mr. Smith, Richard Lambe and Jasper Hawkes. On the north side of the same window is another fine brass with an effigy, inscription and shields of arms to the memory of Edmund Shorediche who died in 1584, and his wife and sixteen children. These two brasses concern the inter-family marriage of sister and brother to brother and sister.

Close by is a slate tablet to Michael Shorediche, who died in 1623, and a black marble tablet with skull and crossbones to the memory of Richard Shorediche, who died in 1660. A black and white oval tablet on the south wall, the scrolls and achievements of arms, are to Robert Shorediche, who died in 1676.

The south window of two lights, with stained glass of "St's Petrus and Paulus", is in memory of Helen Clarke, who died on November 15th, 1895. The east chancel window of three cinque-foiled lights is to the memory of William Capel Clarke-Thornhill. On the west wall beyond the north aisle is a white marble tablet on a black base remarkably inscribed: *"Sacred to the memory of a sincere Christian, Mary, the amiable wife of the Rev. Thomas Clarke of Swakeley. If diligence in the discharge of every Relative and Social Duty; If affection for the poor evinced by the kindest offices of Humanity Can claim Respect and Love. Hers was that claim. She died, Novber the 18th 1771, aged 44. Reader lament not the Dead but the Living."*

In the old vault are memorial tablets to some of those whose bodies were immured within its walls. It will be seen that Sir James Harington had two daughters named Elizabeth. A tablet on the wall reads as follows: *"Within this pillar is enshrined the bodie of Elizabeth Harington second daughter of Sir James Harington of Swakely, Knight and Baronett who felle asleepe in the third yeare of her childhood 7 of Novemb 1647".*

Another tablet in the floor reads: *"Under this marble lieth intoumbed the mayden dust of Elizabeth Harington eighth daughter of Sir James Harington of Swakely in y county of midlesex Knight and Baronett who in y first day of decemb; 1654 and in the sixt yeare of hir childhood fell asleepe."*

A memorial to the brother of Sir Robert Vyner is inscribed: *"Within this Place is immured the Body of THOMAS VYNER ESQ. Executor of Sr. Robert Vyner of Swakely Barronet in which Imployment meeting with great difficulties by the Shutting up of the Exchequer in the reign of KING CHARLES the Second, he so much Impaired his health that for the Recovery thereof he travelled into Italy and died at Rome the six day of December in the year of our Lord 1707. According to his request his Body was Transported to England and deposited here."*

On the West Wall are some tablets recording the death of members of the Clarke family. One is to the memory of John George Clarke, Barrister-at-law, who died in 1800. It bears a figure representing Religion. In one hand the figure holds a book, while the other rests on a coffin partly hidden by a pall. Another pays tribute to *"the Rev. THOMAS CLARKE of Swakely, for nearly 50*

St. Giles' Church 1807, showing the old 'Buntings' at left

years the beloved and venerated pastor of this parish. *In fulfilling the duties of his Station, as in supporting the more enlarged and varied relations of domestic and social life, he exhibited to all who knew him a convincing instance how respectable and how lovely the fallen nature of man is yet capable of appearing when animated by the spirit of genuine Christianity. After a long and almost uninterrupted course of health, cheerfulness and active virtue he fell a victim to the decay of age on the 22nd of Novr MDCCXCVI. AET 75* (1796. Aged 75). *Let me die the death of the righteous and let my last end be like his."*

There are two tablets to the memory of the sons of Thomas Truesdale Clarke and one of them has a strange inscription. It seems that young John Cholmeley Clarke fell from a third floor balcony at Swakeleys. If the father was of the opinion that his son leapt to his death, it would explain the inscription, for in those days the taking of one's own life was regarded as unforgivable. It reads as follows: *"Tributary to the memory alas, of a loved and lovely son, John Cholmeley Clarke. Who died at Swakeleys July 15. 1825. aged 20 years. Thourt gone, but whither? To Heaven, to whom? To God. O hush! A Fathers wish! For shame! Sleep on dear clod."*

The other reads: *"Sacred to the memory of the Rev. George Hawkins Clarke. A man whom all that knew, warmly loved. He died at Swakeleys Janr 13th. 1838, aged 24 years."*

A floor slab in the chancel commemorates the death of another rector of the parish, John Glover, D.D., who died in 1714.

During the restoration, a blocked window was uncovered in the

The Story of Ickenham

north wall immediately below the spire. Pieces of iron, lead and green glass were found among the rubble. Mr. Forsyth was of the opinion that the original window was part of the first church. The bust of the Earl of Essex from the Swakeleys screen stands in this window recess. This bust may have been a form of security, when the font was being used as a tea caddy.

On the south wall is a memorial tablet to the men of the village who gave their lives in the First World War. It is inscribed: *"To the Glory of God and in Honoured Memory of the men who fell in the Great War, 1914-1918."*

The names of these sons of the village follow: Herbert Bunce, Henry T. Clayton, Joseph Dickens, Charles G. Gordon, Thomas M. Harrington, Leonard Humphreys, Beauchamp T. Pell, Kenneth M. Weeden, Montague E. Wilden. Each name is followed by the man's honours, rank and regiment.

A Toc H lamp and an illuminated book recording the names of those who fell in World War II stand on the sill of the Cromwell Window. This window contains fragments of 14th century glass from an earlier window broken, perhaps by Cromwell's followers, in the 17th century.

A brass plaque on the wall beneath the belfry commemorates James Gladdy, *"who for 23 years served this church as clerk and sexton. He died July 1927, aged 65."*

Most of the church furniture is modern and was designed by Clifton Davy, F.R.I.B.A. There is a brass plate to his memory on the west wall. The old pulpit, lectern and pews were of a heavy design and made of pitch pine. The replacements are finely carved and in light oak. The pews were given by Miss Shorediche in memory of her family and its long connection with the parish. The pulpit has this inscription: *"To the glory of God and in memory of the Shorediche family, Lords of the Manor of Ickenham circa 1350 to 1819, and Patrons of the Living circa 1350 to 1743. This pulpit was erected A.D. 1926."* The large table

Ickenham Hall

The Churches

St. Giles' Church about 1900

tomb of the Shorediches can be seen just inside the church gate.

The embroidered kneelers are the work of the ladies of the Embroidery Guild. They depict the arms of the diocese of London and of Eton College, patrons of the living of Ickenham. Also shown are various features of the Church and the historic buildings of the parish.

There was a lectern in the same pleasing design as the pews. It was given to the church by Dame Maude Lawrence in honour of her mother, Harriet Lawrence (1820-1917), wife of Lord Lawrence, the Viceroy of India. Dame Maude Lawrence, who died in 1933, was Director of Women's Establishments at the Treasury. She lived in Ickenham Hall, now part of the Compass Community Arts Centre. Lawrence Drive, Ickenham, is named after her. Her lectern is on loan to the R.A.F. Church at Northolt.

The reredos is *"In memory of Harriet Eliza Sutton, who was called to rest on the 10th January, 1926."* It was given by her youngest daughter, Eliza Woodyear Burr, whose husband was a churchwarden for a number of years.

In the churchyard to the east of the porch is the table tomb of William Turner who died in 1689, and Judith, his wife. Their son, William, was appointed to be Headborough of Ickenham for 1691. This officer, variously called

The Story of Ickenham

Effigy of the Clayton Baby

headborough, chief-pledge, burrow-elder or tything man, held in his hands the civil government of ten families of freeholders, in the same manner as the high-constable had of the hundred. The office was, in fact, that of a sub-constable.

There were a number of timber memorials in various parts of the churchyard, made of locally grown elm and oak. They consisted of a pair of stout, carved posts, about two feet out of the ground, one at each end of the grave. A moulded board, morticed between the posts, bore the inscription, which was painted on an oiled or polished surface. These words did not last long, but the timber stood for many years, until finally the last of them disappeared between the two wars.

Of all the monuments in the Church, the one which has attracted most comment is the sculpture of Sir Robert Clayton's little son, who died a few hours after birth in 1665. The effigy rests on a window sill to the right of the altar.

It is interesting to note that another image of the same child can be seen in the church of St. Mary the Virgin at Bletchingley in Surrey. The child lies between its parents, Sir Robert in his mayoral robes, his wife in a fine dress of the Queen Anne period. The monument commemorates Sir Robert's wife, who died on Christmas Day, 1705, after forty-six years of married life.

Katherine A. Esdaile, in *English Church monuments, 1510-1840,* praises the sculptor, Richard Crutcher; "To have translated the peace of death as shown at Ickenham in 1666 into the living likeness of the short-coated babe of 1707 is a feat of great imaginative power on Crutcher's part."

If Richard Crutcher was able to copy the Ickenham effigy for his work at Bletchingly in 1707, it seems likely that the baby was to be seen in the church before being taken into the darkness of the Swakeleys family vault. How

The Churches

else would Crutcher have seen it? For the vault had no door, as we know. The effigy was probably taken into the vault at the time of some other immurement after Crutcher had seen it. When the wall of the vault was taken down for the last time, the marble baby was resting on the child's coffin. Why it should have been shut away will always remain a mystery, for the inscription indicates that it was meant to be seen.

The Clayton family were staying at Swakeleys when the birth and death occurred. The child is shown in a chrisom cloth. It was the custom in those times for a child to be clad in this white robe to denote its innocence at its baptism. It was then anointed with chrisom oil and the robe placed over the face of the baby. If the child died within a month, the chrisom cloth was used as the burial shroud.

I am indebted to Mr. Bruce Money of Onslow Gardens, London, for the facts concerning the Bletchingly monument. It was Mr. Money who made himself responsible for the restoration of the Clayton Memorial in 1961. The actual work was carried out by Miss Inger Norholt, the sculptress.

The bodies removed from the Swakeleys vault were re-interred in the churchyard. Their names are recorded on the large marble slab covering the grave. The date given is that of the re-interment, 1919. The villagers felt that, since the dead had been evicted from their true resting place, their final grave should be properly marked.

In 1958, the nave was extended, almost doubling the seating capacity of the church. The work of the modern builder married perfectly with the work of the craftsmen of six or seven hundred years ago. A vestry, choir robing room and a toilet were included in the new building. It is difficult to look at the church from inside or outside and convince oneself that it was not all built at the same time.

The one-time vault was put into use as a chapel and dedicated to St. John with a makeshift altar and chairs but at first it was not extensively used. Several pieces of the old pitch pine seats became available in 1978. They were all cut down to a size in keeping with the space and made to seat a dozen people comfortably. The old original altar table was brought into use, and fitted with an oak reredos with three crosses. The plaster work was repaired and painted. All this work was carried out by a local carpenter. St. John's Chapel is frequently used now by the present Rector.

The parish register of Ickenham is in a good state of preservation. Old records of this kind have a fascination and quaintness of their own. The earliest give details of Buryeings 1539-1606, and Crystenyngs 1538-1577. Another contains Cristenings and Buryalles, 1558-1728; Marriages 1558-1732.

The second book carries the following lines:
"This Booke scriptum est James Atlee.
Peruse ths booke with prudencie,
But vewe it not with Momus' eye,   (Momus = Greek god of
I praye you of your curtesie,   ridicule)
Accept my righte good will,
Yf ought herein seeme contrarie
Unto your mynde of fantasie,
Condeame me not to hastelye,   (too hastily)
But blame my want of skill;
Yet as it is receavd, and ther an end,
A worcke well licke of all, is wiselie pend."   (well liked)

37

A third volume records Christenings and burials 1729-1812, but few Marriages. On this account the rector of the day made this note: *"All these several marriages registered from such loose papers as I could find in the old book, A.D. 1747, Thomas Clarke"*. The fourth book contains Marriages and Banns 1754-1812.

The author of an old book entitled *Beauties of England* refers to the Ickenham Parish Register. He observes; *"A branch of the noble family of Hastings formerly resided in the parish"*, and it appears that here *"Katherine the dowghter of the Lord Hastyngs and the Lady his wyff, was borne, the Saterday before our Lady-day the Assumption being the 11 day of August, the Godmother Queen Kateryn, by her debite* (deputy), *beying her sister, one Mr. Harbyrds wyff; the other the Lady Margaret Dugles, the King's nece and the Godfather the Lord Russell beying the Lorde Prive Seale, by hys debite, Master Francis Russell, hys son and heyre 1542."*

This daughter of Lord Hastings, afterwards the Earl of Huntingdon, whose baptism is thus curiously recorded, was married to Henry Clinton, Earl of Lincoln. Anne Parr, daughter of the Marquis of Northampton, and wife of William Herbert, afterwards Earl of Pembroke, is the personage described as *"one Mr. Harbyrds wyff"*.

The entries in the register which may refer to guests or manservants are the following: *"William Morgage from Swaklyse house of this parrysh was buryed vpon XXI day of Aprill in the yere of our lord god 1590. Regno maiestatis XXXII"*. *"1591. Henery Kenryke, alias Williams, deceased at Swakelys house in this parrysh was buryed vpon XXI februarie in the abovesaid."*

Among the recorded marriages appear many quaint spellings of ordinary names: *"Thos. Edmondes, footman to the Queene, of Harveild* (Harefield) *and Jone Yonge 5 Nov. 1558." "Rich. Lambe of St. Bottolffe without Aldergate, and Ann Saye, 24 Feb. 1559." "Raphe Readinge of Ryslypp, and Wenefred Turner, w., 3 Sept. 1561." "Thos. Heylie and ales Adkince, sevants 31 Jan. 1590." "Mr. Nathannell Nicholas, minester, and Mrs. Martha Hamonde of Thistleworth, declared at Woxbridge, 19 Mar. 1656."*

This Nathannell Nicholas is probably the Nathaniel Nicholls mentioned in a Parliamentary Inquiry of 1650. He was rector of Ickenham from 1650 to 1660. In a survey of Church livings at the time of the Commonwealth appears the following entry under the heading of Ickenham: *"Item. —— We present that we have one parsonage in the presentation of Richard Shoreditch, Esq. which with the tithes thereto belonging, twenty-five acres of glebe land, in several fifteen lands in the common fields, and two leets of meadow we value at one-hundred-thirty-eight pounds per annum, and that one Nathaniel Nicholls is our present and constant preaching minister put in by the Honourable Committee for plundered ministers (shortly after the sequestration of Dr. Clare), who has all the aforesaid profits for his salary; and we humbly conceive our said parish too little to be divided, and too big and too far distant to be joined to any other."*

At various times the value of the rectory of Ickenham was rated at £13/6/8 in the old valors, and in the King's books at £16/6/8. (A "valor" was a list of church property, with its value).

Other interesting entries in the parish register are: *"Daniell Spaget, butler to Sir James Harington, and Dority Dabney, servant, published 27 Dec. 1657." "Jeremiah Semer and Joanna Cemkine, declared 3 Oct. 1658."*

The christenings of the children of Sir James Harington are included in volume two: "*William, son of Sir James Harington and Catherine his wife, baptized June 7, 1647.*" "*Lucy their daughter, May 7, 1648.*" "*Catherine Eliza, Aug. 9. 1655.*"

According to an old document quoted in Redford and Riches' *History of Uxbridge* a Lecturer was appointed at the Chapel of Uxbridge, in the parish of Hillingdon in the county of Middlesex. A house was built for his benefit, but the funds were insufficient and the Lecturer had to pay off the mortgage himself. Thereafter the Lecturer was "obliged to keep and maintain the same in good repair, and also to teach six poor boys of Uxbridge aforesaid in reading and writing. And in case the Lecturer of Uxbridge for the time being shall refuse to teach the six poor boys, then the said Lecturer shall pay or cause to be paid unto the Chapel-Wardens of Uxbridge, the sum of Six pounds of lawful English money yearly and every year, to defray the teaching of the six poor boys."

With reference to the Lecturer's appointment, the following is an extract from the Vestry Minute Book: "*Wee the Chapell Wardens and Overseers of the Poor of the Towne of Vxbridge, and others the Inhabitants of the same Towne, Att a Vestry held for the Towne of Vxbridge aforesaid, this Tenth day of June, Anno Dni. 1718, Doe Elect and Choose the Reverend Mr. John Shoreditch, Rector of Ickenham, in the county of Middlesex, to be Lecturer of the said Towne of Vxbridge, to preach the Afternoone Lector every Sunday, or to cause or procure a Minister to preach the same, in the Chappell belonging to the said Towne, and to receive and take the moneys Gathered in the said Towne, for preaching the afternoone Lector aforesaid, and to live in the house in Cowly Field, and have the Benifitt of the School there, he only being subject to such payments as the Reverent Mr. Jaquies deceased our late Minister was subject unto. And We doe hereby agree, that the said Reverent Mr. John Shoreditch shall be the Lecturer, and enjoy the Subscription house and Schoole aforesaid, in the same manner and as fully as the Reverend Mr. Jaquies aforesaid, deceased, in his lifetime Enjoyed the same. Witness our hands.*"

The declaration is signed by John Wolfe, Vicar of Hillingdon, Michael Ravis and Nich. Brown, Chappel wardens, John Battey, Leonard Battersby, Rob. Redman, Araall (sic) Allen, W. Haynes and John Clench, overseers, and the signatures of thirty-three other townsmen.

In the year 1796, the only surviving member of the Trustees of the Parsonage House, the Rev. Thomas Clarke, rector of Ickenham, passed away. His son Thomas Truesdale Clarke of Swakeleys became possessed of the property as heir at law of his late father.

THE RECTORS OF ST. GILES' CHURCH

John Payne 1335. John de Brothampton 1353-1382. John Philipp 1382-1399. John Bradeley 1399-1401. John de Thorp 1401. Stephen Riordenere 1411. Robert Wakefield 1411-1433. William Cornish 1433-1441. John More 1441-1444. John Spygurnell 1444-1452. Thomas Vesey 1452-1454. Robert Haysand 1454-1455. John Goffe 1455-1457. George Bastwick 1457-1459. Thomas Peny (alias Chandler) 1459-1462. Richard Child 1462-1463. James Derwent 1463-1464. John Sawier 1464-1482. Miles Beckwith 1482-1486. George Percy (alias Gard) 1486. Richard Roston 1486-1488. Thomas Goodwyn 1488-1501. William Wright 1501-1531. THE REFORMATION, 1529. John Dyer 1531-1568. Sir Henry Kendall 1568-1624. Robert Say 1624-1626. Lancelot Harrison 1626 ... Andrew Cleere (or Dr. Clare) 1635-1650. Nathaniel Nicholls 1650-1660. William Bere (or Bird)

The Story of Ickenham

1660-1685. John Glover 1686-1714. John Shorediche 1714-1725. Samuel Gilman 1725. Henry Jodrell 1725-1747. Thomas Clarke 1747-1796. Henry Dearman 1796-1800. Thomas Bracken 1800-1815. John Addison 1815-1859. Beauchamp Henry St. John Pell 1859-1907. William Bury, Canon of Peterborough, 1908-1919. Hugh B. Langton 1919-1923. Douglas W. W. Carmichael 1923-1933. James King 1933-1949. Frederick J. Evans 1949-1959. Percy Kingston 1959-1964. Archie Markby 1964-1968. Victor B. Wynburne 1968-1977. Paul M. H. Kelly 1977 ...

Non-conformity in Ickenham dates from 1831, when William Brickett and his wife invited some friends to join them in Sunday evening prayers at their cottage in Glebe Lane. The Bricketts had been worshippers at Providence Congregational Church, Uxbridge, and were encouraged by its Deacons to begin services in Ickenham. The Bricketts' cottage proved too small for the numbers who wished to attend. Clearly, a chapel was needed.

With the concurrence of the Lord of the Manor, three Providence Deacons were made tenants of a piece of waste ground belonging to Ickenham Manor. The record of the transaction runs as follows: *"Edward Brown of Uxbridge in Middlesex, in consideration of five pounds paid by George Hethering-*

The United Reformed Church

The Churches

ton of Uxbridge in the county of Middlesex, grocer, Henry Morten of Hillingdon End, in the same county, builder, William Nash, of the same place, baker, surrenders into the hands of the Lord of the Manor of Ickenham all that piece or parcel of land formerly part of the manor, containing from south to north one hundred and fifty feet, from east to west in a straight line at right angles to the road thirty feet. The same more or less abutting north and west Ickenham Green, east on the highway road leading from Ickenham to Ruislip, and south on footpath next the feeder with the appurtenances and to which said Edward Brown was admitted at a General Court holden for this Manor on the 20th day of October 1834. Proclamation made and court discharged."

The chapel was built at a cost of £160. It was a small, plain brick building, covered in cement mortar to hide structural flaws, with pointed "Gothick" windows. It opened on November 3rd, 1835, when the Reverend John Hunt of Brixton preached the first sermon. Over the years, the increasing congregation, particularly Sunday School pupils, made additions necessary. In 1861 a schoolroom annexe was built and in 1921 a much larger wooden hall rose at the rear of the chapel.

In the early days, ordinary working people used to walk from Ickenham to Uxbridge and back to attend services. William Brickett's son, David, would be sent off on a Sunday morning to Providence Church, Uxbridge, carrying his lunch in a large red handkerchief. After lunch, he would walk back to Ickenham for afternoon Sunday School and evening service. The first Sunday School Superintendent, James Geary, was another indefatigable walker. From 1849 to 1879, he walked every Sunday from Uxbridge to Ickenham. Villagers used to say they could set their clocks by him.

David Brickett subsequently became a pillar of the Congregational Church and was highly respected in the area. During the celebrations for Edward VII's coronation, he was made responsible for the good behaviour of the Irish navvies, who were in Ickenham to build the Metropolitan Railway. His influence prevented any disturbances. He died in 1904, aged 74, and a memorial tablet to him can be seen in the present church.

In 1919, Ickenham finally became fully independent from Providence Church, Uxbridge, but it was not until 1927 that the church had a full-time Deacon. With the rapid growth of Ickenham in the late 1920s, the little chapel in the High Road had become over-crowded. From September, 1930, the village hall was hired for services. Oddly enough, the chapel had never been licensed for marriages. Not till November, 1930, when it was no longer used for services, was a wedding solemnised there.

A new church was now badly needed. A site was bought in the Rectory Field, Swakeleys Road. The new building was opened and dedicated on October 7th, 1936, and has been in continuous use ever since, except on a few occasions during the last War, when fear of air-raids led to morning services being held in the cellars of the Old Rectory. In 1953, a new hall with seating for 200 was opened, and has proved a great asset for concerts and meetings.

Those who work for the church today are too many to mention individually. However, no record of the Free Church movement would be complete without the names of some of those who contributed so much in the early days: such ardent workers as the Saiches, the Claytons, the Randalls, the Taylors, the Bunces, the Weatherleys and the Marriages, not forgetting the Moons and Harrisons from Ruislip. The author remembers particularly 'Ike'

41

The Story of Ickenham

Collins, a lay preacher loved by young and old alike, and the Reverend F. L. Riches Lowe of Providence Church, Uxbridge, whose visits to his friends at Ickenham were always red letter days.

LIST OF MINISTERS

E. A. Willis	1927-1932
William C. Franklin	1932-1934
J. R. Ackroyd	1941-1944
E. J. James	1944-1952
G. F. Barrow	1952-1962
Donald Howell	1962-1972
R. Boulter	1972-1978
A. O. Cassingham	1978-

Chapter Five
Law and Disorder

Early legal records often reflect the intolerance that characterised English religious life for centuries. One aspect of this intolerance was the punishment imposed on people who did not attend an Anglican church for Sunday worship. For this offence, they would be tried at the Middlesex County Sessions held in Hickes Hall, Clerkenwell. If the charge was proved, the offender would either pay a fine or spend time in the stocks or pillory, enduring public humiliation.

Here is a typical entry from the records of the County Sessions: *"23 June, 26 Elizabeth (1584). For not going to church, chapel or any place of Common Prayer, from the said 23 June 26 Elizabeth to 28 Sept then next following, Bernard Brocas of Ickenham, Co. Middx, was found to be guilty"*. (G.D.R. 5 Oct. 26 Elizabeth.) (G.D.R = Gaol Delivery Roll.)

Another found guilty at the same time was Elizabeth Waters, wife of "Richard Waters, of Ickenham, Co. Middx. gentleman". She was found guilty on a similar charge the next year. The punishment is not recorded. Perhaps it had some effect, for she did not appear at the Court for three years after the second judgement. Then both she and her servant, Margaret, were charged with non-attendance and found guilty.

An officer called the Petty Constable (usually just Constable) was responsible for keeping the peace in the village. Over him were the two High Constables of the Hundred of Elthorne. The word "constable' comes from the Latin 'comes stabuli" (count of the stable). In Ickenham, the Constable was often a member of the Crosyer, Osmond or Turner families. In 1613, Robert Crosyer was Constable and in 1617 it was Richard Osmond. Both styled themselves "gentleman", meaning above the rank of yeoman (small farmer). The constable, also called headborough, had responsibility for gathering tithes and other money or merchandise due to the parish church. In 1691, the records show John Turner and John Gravett succeeding William Gravett and John Marlowe, yeomen, as headboroughs for Ickenham. The office of constable persisted for many years until the County Police Acts of 1839 and 1840 made it possible for certain justices to establish a paid police force.

Another long-lived institution was the Court Baron. It dealt with the affairs of the manor such as land encroachment, non-payment of dues and the neglect of property rented from the manor by the tenants. It was often held at the manor house with the lord presiding over his assembled tenants (known as the Homage). In Ickenham during the 19th century, 'The Coach and Horses' became the venue for the Court Baron; the last to be held there was in 1878.

Old court records make quaint and fascinating reading. Here are some extracts relating to Ickenham:

1411. *"William Legette hath a tanhouse, formerly of Reginald Affelde, and permits same to be ruinous. Therefore he in mercy, and it is ordered that he repair it against the next Court under pain of 40 shillings."*

43

The Story of Ickenham

Ickenham showing the 'Coach and Horses' about 1910

The phrase "in mercy" often appears in manorial records and means that a tenant had failed in his duties and was dependent on the clemency of his lord. William Legette was often in trouble, it seems:

"*At this court came William Legette and Margery his wife, she being separately examined, and surrendered into the hands of the Lord one tenement with certain parcels of land called Reynold's Haffolds. To the use of John Goldyng and his heirs, whereupon then happenith to the Lord 2d.*"

1524. "*It was presented that Thomas Nelham had one small ditch not sufficiently scoured nor made and one hedge in like Condition lying between the Croft and Wilbersouth to the damage of the Lord's tenants there. Therefore it is commanded to the said Thomas that he repair the said ditch and hedge against the Feast of the Annunciation of the Blessed Virgin Mary under the pain of the forfeiture of forty shillings.*"

There is a record of a riot in 1563. The Constable would have been helpless against a disturbance of this size: "*True bill that at Ickenham in the county of Middlesex on the 25th of July 1563, John Smyth, gentleman, Edmund Smyth, Gentleman, Robert Beringer, yeoman, Thomas Vyncent, laborer, Robert Upton, laborer, James Durenger, laborer, Richard Herne, yeoman, Richard Cluck, laborer, George Dovey, laborer, Richard Chambre, laborer, Robert Stanbridge, Carpenter, John Herne, laborer, John ....., Husbandman, Amphilisia Lewell, spinster, Alice Adams, widow, Isabel Hale, spinster, all late of Ryslippe, in the county of Middlesex, and Goodluck Drawater, laborer, Thomas Smyth, laborer, John Adams, laborer, William Waite, laborer, John Smyth, laborer, Isabel Smyth, spinster, and Margaret Exton, spinster, assembled in warlike manner, and broke riotously into the close of William Say, gentleman, and unlawfully carried away four wainloads of wheat there late growing belonging to the said William Say, and worth twelve pounds". (G.D.R. 6 Elizabeth).*

The "True Bill" mentioned above was a bill of indictment endorsed, after investigation, by a grand jury as containing a case for the court.

"26th of August 1569. True bill that on the said day and at other times before and afterwards Matthew Vincent of Ickenham in the county of Middlesex, not having lands, tenements, rents or service to the value of 40s a year, kept and used dogs for coursing hares, nets, ferrets, and dogs for chasing by scent, and further that he in company with others broke at Hillingdon, co. Middlesex into the free warren of Edward, Earl of Darbie, and there hunted the rabbits of the said Earl." (General Session of Peace Roll. Michaelmas II Elizabeth.)

"A true bill was found that on the 14th day of December in the 8th year of the reign of James I, Edward Newdigate, gentleman, and William Smyth, yeoman, both late of London, stole a graye geldinge worth five pounds, a graye mare worth fifty shillings and a white leather saddle worth five shillings of the goods and chattels of William Cragge gentleman. William Smyth was at large. Edward Newdigate was found to be guilty and sentenced to be hung." (G.D.R. Dec. 8 James I).

At the time of this case William Cragge was the tenant of Swakeleys and was himself the subject of a lawsuit brought against him by the owner, John Bingley, in 1616. (See Chapter 3).

"13 January, II James I, 1614. Richard Nelham of Ickenham in the county of Middlesex, yeoman, and John .... of Rislipp for William Kinton of the same, yeoman, to answer for touching and carrying away of certain wood being the goods of John Winchester of Tylehouse in Rislipp aforesaid." ("John .... of Rislipp" was a man of some learning representing William Kinton.)

As well as dealing with major crimes and offences, the County Court also issued various licences. The Court granted a licence for Badgers, Kidders and Drovers to "Michael Shoreditche of Ickenham, in Middlesex, gentleman," on the 15th of April, 1613. This enabled him to deal in corn and cattle. (A "badger" or "kidder" was a middle man, who would buy corn, fish, butter or cheese from the producers and sell them at market elsewhere.)

"Recognizence taken at Hickes Hall in Clerkenwell, before Sir William Waad, (sic) *Knight, Justice of the Peace, and nine other Justices of the Peace, of Michael Shoreditche, of Ickenham, gentleman, in the sum of one hundred pounds. For the good behaviour of the said Michael Shoreditche brought before the same Justices to answer 'for speakinge divers unfitt and mutynous speeches touching a rate made by His Majestyes Justices of the Peace for the making of a House of Correccion, namely that the County would withstande the rate." (3 December, II James I, 1615.)* (At an earlier hearing, in 1614, he had attended the Sessions and had been discharged. Francis Blackwell of Ickenham, husbandman, also came and was discharged for good behaviour.)

It was charged that *"at Woxbridge, co. Middlesex, Thomas Smyth of Wenloxbarne, co. Middlesex, yeoman, one of the Queen's takers and providers for wains and carts for ale and beer, by colour of his office took extortionatelye five shillings of John Osmond, for the exoneration of the said John Osmond's wain, and also on the same day and in the same way he took and extorted thirteen shillings and eightpence at Ickenham co. Middlesex, from Thomas Nelham and six shillings and eightpence at Ickenham from the aforenamed John Osmond."* The prisoner, Thomas Smyth, was found to be guilty.

The Story of Ickenham

Thomas Gibbons, a yeoman of Ickenham, was sworn in as Constable of the parish in the place of William Osmond on the 26th of May in 1661. In the same year, an order was made for William Turner to be headborough for the same parish.

An entry dated April, 1692, reads "Upon the petition of Thomas Gibbons, constable of Ickenham, showing that he has served the office for the past year, and that there was no court leet held for the said parish last Easter, and praying that he might be discharged from serving the said office, and that John Turner, of Ickenham, gentleman, might be elected in his place."

Three years later, the following appeared: "The appointment has been made of treasurer, of John Turner, of Ickenham, gentleman, for the Hundreds of Elthorne, Spelthorne, Isleworth, in the place of John Smith, Gentleman, April, 1695."

The first reference to the Turner family concerned one of their workers. In the Court Baron of 1411, it was presented that the manservant of Thomas Turner "broke the Lord's pound and let divers cattle escape from the said pound after they were impounded, to the great damage of the Bailiff, therefore he in mercy. Also that the wife of William Atte Lee carried away fuel from the Lord's wood and broke the Lord's hedges, therefore she in mercy."

The Lord of the Manor was empowered to impound cattle on his own account. Animals so taken from a tenant because he was behind with his rent, were fed and the cost added to the debt of the defaulting tenant.

At a Court Baron in 1731, John Weeden, a farmer of Denham in Buckinghamshire, was admitted as a tenant farmer by Richard Shorediche, Lord of Ickenham, before Jabez Goldar. This was the beginning of the Weeden family's long association with the village. Among the farms occupied by Weedens through the years have been Long Lane Farm, Beetonswood Farm and Church Farm. The Weedens took over as the Turners and Osmonds faded from the village scene. They held many parish appointments. James Weeden the younger was Bailiff to the Manor and Charles became Clerk to the Parish Council. In 1828, it is recorded that "Charles Weeden, the parish Clerk, refused to read the notice of a Court Baron without a fee of one shilling to which he was entitled for such service."

When the first Parish Council elected under the Local Government Act of 1894 met for the first time, George Weeden was one of its members. The others who formed the council were David Brickett, Benjamin Johnson, Algernon Saich, Joseph Sims and Henry George Weatherley. They met for the first time on the 17th of December in 1894. The following year, Henry Weeden was appointed as an Overseer of the Council. It was his duty to bring to the notice of the Council nuisances which might have occurred within the parish from time to time, and to see to the administration of the Poor Law.

In April, 1903, George Weeden was elected as Chairman of the Council. He held this position until 1908, when he resigned as a member of the Council, in order to apply for the post of Clerk of the Parish Council. He held this appointment until 1926. Reginald Weeden had been elected to the Council in 1924. He and his uncle George remained in their respective posts until the Parish Council ceased to exist by Act of Parliament, the duties thereafter being carried out by the Uxbridge Urban District Council.

While men such as the Turners and the Weedens were ensuring that the parish ran smoothly, others were going their own way in blissful ignorance of laws and precedents. There are always a few misfits, eccentrics and non-conformists, even in a place as small as Ickenham. They make life more interesting for the rest. Ickenham has had several colourful characters, none more so than Roger Crab.

The *Dictionary of National Biography* summarises what is known about Crab. He was born in Buckinghamshire around 1621 and, by the age of twenty, had adopted a rigorously vegetarian diet, excluding even cheese and butter. He never drank anything stronger than water. He was a religious mystic, who considered himself "above ordinances, though sympathising with neither Leveller nor Quaker."

In 1642, he began seven years' service in the Parliamentary army, fighting against Charles I. Whilst serving, he not only continued with his strange vegetarian diet but induced others to follow him. One of his disciples was a Captain Norwood. The Captain died, perhaps because of his frugal fare.

During his service, Crab was sentenced to death on the battlefield by "my Lord Protector" but the sentence was commuted to two years' imprisonment. He left the army in 1649 "with a skull cloven to the brain by an adversary's sword during the fighting." He then opened a haberdashery in Chesham. He stayed there two years, after which his views on life went through another change by illumination. Digging in his garden with his face towards the East, he saw "the Paradise of God". He sold his shop in Chesham and gave the proceeds to the poor. He settled on a "small rood of ground at Icknam, near Uxbridge," for which he paid fifty shillings a year. There he lived in a house of his own building.

Crab professed to be a physician, astrologer and seer. Amongst other things, it is said that he foretold the Restoration in 1660 and the accession to the throne of England by William of Orange in 1688. As a physician, he claimed to have had "a hundred or six score patients at once."

In 1654, Crab went to London to supervise the publication of his book, *The English hermit, or wonder of this age*. The title continues for more than a hundred words! In it Crab claims to have cut his living expenses to three farthings a week. He lived mostly on cabbages, turnips, carrots, dock leaves and grass, and clothed himself in sack cloth.

Before his conversion, Crab *"transgressed the commands of God"* and was *"guilty of the whole law, living in pride and drunkenness and gluttony,"* which he *"upheld by dissembling and lying, cheating and cozening my neighbours."* Then he repented and set out to punish his body, which had led him astray through fleshly desires. *"And instead of strong drinks and wines, I gave the old man a cup of water and, instead of roast mutton and rabbits and other dainty dishes, I gave him broth thickened with bran, pudding made with bran, turnip leaves chopped together and grass. At which the old man (meaning my body) being moved, would know what he had done that I used him so hardly. Then I showed him his transgressions, as aforesaid. So the fleshly members rebelled against the laws of my mind and had a shrewd skirmish but the mind, being well enlightened, held it. So the old man grew sick and weak with the flesh like to fall to the dust but the wonderful love of God (well pleased with the battle) raised him up again and filled him full of love and peace and content in mind, and is now become more humble for now he will eat dock leaves, mallows and grass."*

Crab recommends poverty by quoting the words of Christ, *"...Go thy way; sell whatever thou hast and give to the poor, and thou shalt have treasure in Heaven..."* He justifies vegetarianism by a strange argument, claiming that, as the

The Story of Ickenham

> Roger Crab, that feeds on Hearbs and Roots is here,
> But I believe Diogenes had better Cheer.   Rara avis in terris.

> Deep things more I have to tell, but I shall now forbeare:
> Left some in wrath against me swell, and do my body teare.

Roger Crab, the Ickenham Hermit

receiver of stolen goods is always worse than the thief, the eater of meat or the drinker of wine must always be worse than the butcher or the publican.

    Whilst in London to publish *The English Hermit* Crab again fell foul of authority. He was arrested for Sabbath-breaking, tried at the Middlesex County Sessions, and committed to Clerkenwell Prison. He records that his keeper brought him no food, his only meal being a crust of bread brought to him by a dog. After his release, and the publication of his book, he returned to live his

Law and Disorder

monastic type of life at Ickenham.

Roger Crab was obviously a much persecuted man, probably not so much for what he did as for the views which he held. In those days, people with power were intolerant of those who held opinions which did not fit in with their own, and they punished them. Today the intolerance is still with us but not the power to punish. Crab records that a minister of Uxbridge, named Godbold, denounced him as a male witch and said he should be burned at the stake.

Wiser counsels prevailed and he was not burned. He was whipped on occasion for Sabbath-breaking and spent many hours in the stocks.

He went to London again in 1657 on another publishing venture. The book was entitled *Dagons Downfall, or The Great Idol digged up Root and Branch*. In this work he occasionally lapsed into rhyme:

> "Deep things more I have to tell
> But I shall now forebeare,
> Lest some in wrath against me swell,
> And do my body teare."

> "When I was a digging parsnips
> For my meals,
> Then I discovered these cheats
> For which I sate six houres by the heels."

Crab eventually moved to Bethnal Green and remained there till his death. He was buried in the precincts of Stepney Parish Church. His tombstone, which is now a paving slab, may be seen but the inscription is almost unreadable. It was as follows: "*Here remains all that was mortal of Mr. Roger Crab, who entered into eternity the 11th day of September, 1680, in the 60th year of his age.*"

In more modern times Ickenham was the home of another hermit. He, too, lived in a house of his own building. Philip Woodley, known to everyone as "Chunky", lived in the overgrown lane to the west of Breakspear Road, opposite the western entrance to Ickenham Green. His home was made with sacks, pieces of tarpaulin, sheets of metal and anything else which might keep out the rain and wind. The shack was propped up with saplings.

Chunky wore many coats. Indeed, when he sallied forth to do his shopping, all his worldly goods, except his kettles and saucepans, could be carried in his pockets. In wet weather, the weight of his sodden garments made him walk even slower than usual. The bulk of his coats stood out like boards.

Chunky had once been a working man, but, in the late 1920s, after losing his job, he left home and family to become a hermit. He maintained his independence by doing casual hedging and ditching jobs for farmers. He would talk to anybody who passed his hut.

When Chunky walked into the village, he always made his presence felt. He ignored the traffic. Cars would slow and halt, the drivers staring in amazement as he plodded across the road with a devilish mischief in his eyes. If a car came too close, Chunky would blaze with rage and consign all motorists to perdition. Ladies who remarked, no matter how quietly, on his filthy appearance would find to their embarrassment that his ears, at least, did not need washing. They would get the length of his tongue.

But the old hermit did have some friends. They were the birds that hopped in and out of his hut and shared his meals. When a Sunday newspaper

49

The Story of Ickenham

published an article on Chunky before the last war, it included a photograph of the old man with birds perched beside him and on his table. He died a few years after the War.

For a while, Chunky had neighbours almost as disreputable as himself. Yorky Simmons and his Romany wife had set up camp in the entrance to the Green on the other side of Breakspear Road. They had a caravan and a wagon with a tarpaulin stretched between the two.

Yorky and his wife would not have been able to stay so long in the days when Ickenham's affairs were run by the parish council. At that time, gypsies and travellers were allowed to camp for one night at the bottom end of the Green. If they stayed longer, P.C. Jim Hall would pay them a visit. Those who did not know him might be prepared to argue, but they never did it twice. At the sight of his burly figure approaching, horses would be caught and put in the shafts ready for a quick getaway.

But Yorky came to Ickenham when the local authority was in Uxbridge. So he was able to stay on and raise a family. He was frequently summoned for failing to send his children to school. Not that he cared. He would just grin, displaying the gap in his top front teeth.

Yorky made his living by selling fire logs, by carting odds and ends from one place to another, and by other small bits of business. But he was always ready to stop for a chat. He liked to talk about the army and Spion Kop (a notable battle of the Boer War).

He was once charged at Uxbridge Court with putting his donkeys to graze on land owned by the Great Western Railway Company. The land was completely enclosed by a barbed wire fence and it was a mystery how Yorky had managed to get inside. The company decided to set a 24 hour watch. What they saw filled them with amazement and a certain amount of respect for Yorky.

Yorky was seen to approach the enclosure with his donkeys. Somehow, whether by tripping, pushing or cajoling, he got the first animal to lie on its side. Then he crawled under the wire and dragged the donkey after him. The performance was repeated with the other two donkeys. Yorky was caught red-handed. He gave his toothy grin and did not try to deny it.

Like all travellers, Yorky finally moved on. He was seen in Ruislip and then in Buckinghamshire and then he was lost to view. He stayed longer than most vagrants and was better known. Before the last War, tramps were a common sight in the village but they rarely stayed more than a few days. Most of them were amiable enough. They were known by nicknames which the children had bestowed upon them. Most passed through at regular intervals, probably doing a round of the workhouses of the day.

They would knock on a door (they had a grapevine, too,) and were rarely turned away. The request was usually the same: *"Ask yer mother t'fill this with 'ot water, please. Tell 'er the tea's inside it."*

The can was just an old tin, holding about a pint, with a piece of wire strung across the top for a handle. The tramp would then sit on the door-step or by the pump to await a call. When it came, the tramp's tea had been replaced by some more in a little bag. It would be accompanied by a slice of bread and dripping or a chunk of cake or bread pudding, even though the family could ill afford it. The men were always so grateful.

The children were fond of some tramps, scared of others. They all loved Sailor, who made ships in bottles. He sometimes gave them away when he

Law and Disorder

thought the wistful child came from a poor family. But selling the model ships was his means of making a few pence. After spending a day or two around the village, he might be seen making his way into a spinney for his night's sleep. In the morning he'd be gone, leaving not a trace to show he'd been there.

Flowery Dick, a gaunt, ageless man with long flowing hair and beard, instilled a certain amount of fear into some of the younger ones. Some were imprudent enough to call after him as they went to school. The old man resented it and went to the school to make his protest to the headmaster. "Why can't they leave an old soldier alone?" he asked. "Why not, indeed?" said Mr. Lee, and invited him into the school.

Standing by the old man, who had taken his hat off, Mr. Lee told the class about rudeness and small-mindedness, lecturing them on their behaviour. He then drew back the old soldier's coat to reveal a row of medals. No one forgot that lesson, and thereafter, if anyone spoke to Flowery Dick, it was with respect. He was so called from his way of making flowers from the pith of water rushes. When handed his tea, he always gave his benefactor a spray of these artificial flowers.

A small knight of the road, known as Loopy, carved knives and forks from solid pieces of wood. These were not crudely made, as one might expect, but finished with real skill. Loopy sold his work for a few coppers. Such men stayed a few days and then were gone.

Quite another type were the "diddy-kies". Neither gypsies nor show-folk, they travelled in caravans crudely made by bending a sheet of metal into a hoop over a wagon. They were the most unwelcome visitors. Their income was derived from making wooden clothes pegs and props which they sold from door to door. The wood for these pegs was often stolen. Many a venturesome chicken has found its way into their old iron pots.

Chapter Six

Philanthropy and Education

"The evil that men do lives after them; the good is oft interred with their bones." This could not apply to Charlotte, the wife and widow of John Henry Gell, of Buntings. The good she did while she lived, lives on, and so does the good which she bequeathed after her death. She loved the pleasure which her generosity gave to the people of the village. Many of the prizes at the fair were due to her kindness and its influence on other wealthy residents. But most of her benevolence was of a more substantial form.

Several years before her death, she had a row of flint and red brick cottages built on her land in Back Lane (Swakeleys Road). The land adjoined the orchard and kitchen garden of Buntings. Over the front door of the middle cottage is the inscription "Ickenham Cottages". It is strange that, while she lived, she objected to their being referred to as almshouses, yet in her will that is what she called them. She built them to serve the same purpose as the "Grace and Favour" homes at Windsor Castle; that is, to provide homes for her aged and retired servants and their descendants.

Each cottage has a large garden at the back, divided only by footpaths. A common footpath extends completely around the row. Originally, each cottage had its own back door, but the two end pairs shared a front door and staircase.

Mrs. Gell set aside a substantial sum of money which she invested in railway stock. The income from this endowment fund was to be used on the upkeep of the property, and to pay each tenant the weekly sum of eight shillings. The tenant paid back one penny as rent in order to avoid the use of the word 'almshouse'. If two persons were permitted to share a cottage, an extra two shillings per roof should be given to them. In her will, Mrs. Gell directed that her executors should pay to the trustees of her cottages a further sum of £1,000, the income from its careful investment to be devoted to the well-being of the tenants, as she had directed when the endowment fund was first invested.

The rules and regulations governing the Ickenham Cottages, as drawn up by Mrs. Gell and her appointed trustees, were as follows:-

1. Each of the five dwellings, with the garden to be appropriated thereto, may be occupied by a married couple, or by two persons either unmarried, widows or widowers, and at the request of the respective inmates, the trustees shall be at liberty, if they think fit, to allow a third person to live in each dwelling; but no more than three persons shall reside in one dwelling at the same time under any circumstances whatever. Such third person shall be permitted as a lodger only during the pleasure of the trustees, and shall not be entitled to any of the pecuniary benefits provided for the inmates.

2. No male inmate to be admitted under the age of 65 years, and no female under 60 years, but a married couple shall be admitted if one of them shall be qualified as to age. Every inmate must be a member of the Church of England

Philanthropy and Education

and of good character and honest report, and must have pursued some industrious calling for his livelihood. In the election of candidates any person who shall have lived in Mr. or Mrs. Gell's family for five years and persons connected with the parish of Ickenham shall be preferred.

    3. Every inmate shall be required to keep his or her dwelling and garden in clean and neat order; to have the chimneys swept once in every three months, and generally to observe such regulations as the trustees may from time to time make for the cleanliness of the dwellings with regard to health.

    4. No fixtures shall be altered or removed, nor shall any be added without the previous consent of the trustees. Substantial repairs are to be effected by the trustees, out of the fund provided for the purpose, but inmates shall be required to make good all defects and damage caused by their own carelessness or neglect, and failing this, the trustees shall be at liberty to deduct the cost out of the allowances to such defaulting inmate.

    5. Every married couple and every other inmate shall pay to the trustees one penny for rent, and shall, on being admitted, sign an agreement in such form as the trustees shall require, for the care and maintenance of their dwellings and appurtenances, and for the observance of these rules and regulations.

    6. None of these dwellings shall be used as a shop, or for any other purpose than a dwelling, and no inmate shall receive parochial relief.

    7. There shall be paid to the inmates an allowance for their maintenance at the rate of £20 per annum for each house by monthly or such

The Gell Almshouses

The Story of Ickenham

payments as the trustees shall from time to time think fit. Such an allowance of £20 per house to be paid to the husband of a married couple, and to be equally divided between other inmates where there shall be two in one house; or where any house shall be occupied by one inmate only, then the whole of the allowance at the rate of £20 per annum to be paid to such one inmate.

8. In the event of the income of the fund provided for these allowances proving, from unforeseen causes, insufficient in any year to pay the whole, then the inmates shall be subject to a rateable deduction, and in the event of there being a surplus of the income from dwellings being vacant or otherwise, absolute discretion is given, either to accumulate such surplus by adding it to the capital of the endowment or to apply it to any good and charitable cause in the parish of Ickenham. The same liberty and discretion shall be exercised over any excess of income in subsequent years, whether arising from the original endowment fund or from any accumulation thereto.

9. These rules and regulations shall be printed and a copy hung in each dwelling; and any inmate who shall not duly and faithfully observe them or who shall be guilty of any misconduct, or after warning from the trustees shall continue any act that the trustees shall consider to be detrimental or an annoyance of other inmates, shall forthwith be dismissed from his or her dwelling, and shall thereupon forfeit all benefit and advantage to which they otherwise would have been entitled.

Mrs. Gell lived for many years at Buntings, where she died on the 14th of November, 1863. The long eastern boundary of her home was the western boundary of the churchyard. She had a private footpath and a gateway between her large house and the church. This path was used by Miss Helen Cochrane in later years when she served the church as organist, and her family lived at Buntings. It should be remembered that there have been two houses called Buntings. The older one was the home of Mrs. Gell and of Admiral Sir Arthur Cochrane, after his retirement in 1886. The present Buntings was built in 1920.

The cellars of the original Buntings are now a sunken garden. Some of the trees planted in the grounds were brought from foreign parts by Admiral Cochrane. Many were destroyed by those who knew no better, but one or two still survive. Little Buntings, now owned by Cathcart and Co., Solicitors, was an annexe to Buntings and was often used as a guest house.

The archaeologist Howard Carter was a friend of the Cochrane family and often stayed with them. He worked with Lord Carnarvon on the excavation of the tomb of Tutankhamen. The family of Sir Claude Champion de Crespigny were frequent guests of the Cochranes. There is a memorial tablet on the north wall of St. Giles' Church to one of the de Crespignys.

The big house had a fine range of coachhouses and stables, with living accommodation above. During the 1914-18 war, a cavalry regiment and their horses were billeted in them. Their job was to bale the hay of the local farmers for use by the cavalry regiments on war service. All the local hayricks were confiscated by the War Department. After the war, the coachhouses and stables were converted into private dwellings by the new owner, a Miss Tompson.

In her will, Mrs. Gell left £200 to the rector with the request that it should be spent on the improvement of St. Giles' Church. To her appointed trustees, the Rector, William Edward Hillier, and Charles Weeden the elder, and their executors, administrators and assigns, she left the annual sum of £50, to be held in trust by them to supply coals about Christmas time, to such poor

Philanthropy and Education

Ickenham Green about the turn of the century

inhabitants of the parish as they should select. This bequest has been known through the years as 'The Gift Coals'.

To the father, mother or head of every poor labouring family, who at the time of her death were living in the parish, she left nineteen guineas. This sum, she directed, was to be spent in the purchase of warm bedding or other clothing. Every poor bachelor or spinster who at the time of her decease had attained the age of eighteen years, was to be paid the sum of £5 to be spent for the same purpose.

Mrs. Gell made many bequests to people who had served her and her husband. To an old servant long retired, she left nineteen guineas. Her former maid received £100, and the butler still in her service, £250. To a personal servant whom she called her friend, she gave £500 and specified articles of furniture. The gardener still in her employment was given £150 and all the gardening tools and lights. Old Brown, the retired gardener, was given nineteen guineas. Apart from her gifts to Ickenham, she gave during her lifetime and again in her will, large sums of money to the hospitals at Brompton, Westminster and Charing Cross, as well as to a number of Missionary Societies.

This benefactress left directions for her trustees to have a pump built and a deep well sunk on a site convenient for the majority of the villagers. No specified sum of money was mentioned for this, but it was made clear that the trustees should spend whatever they thought necessary to enable them to carry out her wishes. After her death, the pump was built on one of the grass verges near her home. The letter 'G' is incorporated in the weathervane which surmounts the picturesque octagonal roof, with its four dormer windows and ornamental rails. Around the inside of the carved roof plate is this inscription: *"This well was sunk and the pump erected by the Executors of the late Charlotte*

55

The Story of Ickenham

Gell, widow, who died on the 14th of November, 1863, after a long residence in this parish. Mrs. Gell, by her will, desired that this pump should be dedicated to the use of the inhabitants of this village for ever. Erected in the year 1866."

Until the pump was built, many of the villagers had no water supply of their own. They were dependant upon their more fortunate neighbours who had a well or a pump. These were usually only to be found at the farms and larger houses. Until the present pond was dug to take the inevitable waste from the pump, the village pond had been on the south side of the village. It was filled with the earth dug from the new one. When the village was agricultural, homeward-bound horses and cows were wont to quench their thirsts from its water before passing on. Ducks and geese from neighbouring cottages and farms were a part of the village scene. At that time, apart from the roads running through, the rest of the village was greensward. The children used one of the larger pieces on which to play a game very popular throughout the years. It was baseball or rounders, which the Pilgrim Fathers took to their new home in America.

When the affairs previously undertaken by the parish councils were taken over to be managed, or in the case of the outlying villages, mismanaged, by the larger councils, strange things were done in the name of 'progress'. It was decreed by the powers based at Uxbridge that the pond should be filled in and the pump removed, so that cars could rush unhindered from Ruislip to Hillingdon, or from Hillingdon to Ruislip. But the new order of things had reckoned without the old order of men, and the true-born sons of Ickenham would have none of it. The pond and pump meant as much to them as the awful and ridiculous Market House meant to the sons of Uxbridge, or Tower Bridge to the sons of London. This steamroller method of local government raised such a storm that the late Major John Kendall, writing under the pen-name he so often used, wrote the following poem which appeared in *Punch* on the 1st of June 1927.

THE SORROWS OF ICKENHAM

The men that dwell in Ickenham are sore of heart and sad;
Bad news has come to sicken 'em and startle them like mad;
For see, the Council's magic wand is lifted – hence their hump –
To sweep away their village pond and raze the parish pump.

The cars that drive through Ickenham demand a wider way
To stimulate and quicken 'em to valour and display,
A task, though simple to the eye, that baffles e'en the best
While still the pond reflects the sky, the pump uprears its crest.

The public sights of Ickenham are moderate and few,
No football home like Twickenham, no royal lands like Kew;
But local eyes grow soft and fond and local bosoms thump
Before the glory of their pond, the grandeur of their pump.

The girls that love in Ickenham regard their men in doubt,
Whether they've got a kick in 'em, or if they're made without;
In waning trust, the maidens throng about each hallowed spot,
And "Will they bow beneath this wrong", they ask themselves, 'or not?"

Philanthropy and Education

Then rise, you men of Ickenham, confront your haughty foes,
Bring out your spuds to stick in 'em, your shovels and your hoes;
Persuade them to a peaceful bond, or fell them with a bump;
Live if you may, with pump and pond, or die for pond and pump.
"Dum-Dum"
(Reprinted here by kind permission of *Punch*)

The battle of 1927 was won without bloodshed. So, too, was the battle of 1954, when a committee organised for the Coronation celebrations found itself with some surplus funds. They bought a three-sided clock and decided to mount it on the eight-sided pump. After a wordy battle in the local press, the powers at Uxbridge conceded that the clock should not be put on the pump. On the day of this great decision, a representative of the Society for the Protection of Ancient Buildings was due to come to Ickenham and then to visit the council at Uxbridge, but a timely 'phone call made the journey unnecessary.

A composite picture had been published to show people just how ridiculous the clock would have appeared had not wiser counsels prevailed. The clock was later incorporated in the County Library building which stands on the site formerly occupied by Orchard Cottage.

EDUCATION

The first known school in Ickenham was a Lancasterian school which in 1819 gave clothing and elementary education to fifty children. Such schools depended on the older or more intelligent children, who were set to teach their fellow pupils.

In the days before State education, schools relied on the generosity and public spirit of the well-to-do. The Clarke family of Swakeleys did much for education in Ickenham. In 1823, Thomas Truesdale Clarke agreed to maintain Ickenham Church of England School and another school at Uxbridge. In 1833, the school was a fee-paying establishment for ten boys and twice that number of girls.

During the same period, there were smaller, short-lived schools in the village. A girls' private school with 12 pupils existed between 1828 and 1833. There was also a dame school held in the front room of Home Farm at a cost of 2d per child per week. This may have been the dame school recorded as having 14 pupils in 1846.

On Thomas Truesdale Clarke's death in 1840, the responsibility for the Church of England school passed to his son, also named Thomas. By 1846, the school had both a schoolroom and a schoolmistress. The next development was a new school building, which went up in 1866, on the waste of Ickenham manor, to the south side of Ickenham High Road. In 1873 this school had 37 pupils and a salaried schoolmistress, who lived in a house next to the schoolroom. The school was financed by subscriptions and school pence, any deficiency to be made good by the owner, Thomas Clarke. As late as 1907 it was still a privately owned school.

The first teacher in the new school, Miss Anne Wilson, was assisted by two monitors, who were selected from the older girls. One was Jane Winch, the other was Emma Filkins. A few weeks after the opening of the school, it was recorded that Miss Clarke, the Squire's daughter, came to school in the morning and gave the first class a dictation lesson. Several days later, *"Emma Filkins is monitor again this week as Jane Winch has been at Swakeleys to work."* *"Only twelve children at school this afternoon, nearly all the others gone to Uxbridge*

57

The Story of Ickenham

Fair". *"Attendance very small this week, a great many children away picking up acorns."*

The acorns were bought by farmers for the feeding of livestock, mainly pigs. The acorn gatherers were paid at so much a bushel taken to the farm. The farmer at Hill Farm had to pay a penny a bushel more, as his farm was more than a mile from the village. Hill Farm is now part of Northolt aerodrome.

One of the duties of the teacher was to make a weekly report on the school activities for the information of the school managers, presumably the rector and the squire, and for the government inspector, who made regular visits in order to see if the attainments of the children were of a high enough standard to warrant a government grant. Quite often the reports would cover a period of several weeks. The last report of 1873 was for the week ending 14th of November and read *"Walter Butler has been Absent for several weeks. I find on enquiry he has been going to Ruislip School".* Family enquiries elicited the fact that Walter had "a heavy line on" with a Ruislip girl.

The first entry for 1874 reads: *"Attendance not very good this week. Two children have bad feet from chilblains, two bad eyes, one had no shoes, and one obliged to stay home to assist her mother."* An unnamed lady visited the school one afternoon to *"look at the girls' needlework and hear the children sing."* Many references were made to visits by members of the Pell and Clarke families to teach various subjects, but there is no evidence to show that these visits were at all regular.

Miss Wilson was soon to realise that Fair Days had a bad effect on attendances. Following her experience of Uxbridge Fair last year, she felt obliged to give a holiday on Ickenham Fair day. It was held only a hundred yards from the school. Teachers found it to be good policy to give official holidays on all fair days and when the circus was at Uxbridge. Other reasons for bad attendance at various times were:- *"None of the little ones could come today as the snow was too deep." "Sarah Norman has been home for a month taking care of her brother and sister while her mother was at work." 'Could not have school today as the builder was taking down the wall to make a doorway into the classroom which he is building." "The children had their annual tea party at Swakeleys this afternoon." "All the children who do not live in the village and have to pass through it, have been told to stay at home on account of the Scarlet Fever in the village." "Charlotte Milton was re-admitted after being absent for several months, on her promise to attend regularly."* Six weeks later, she left to go into service. *"Ellen Butler away reaping this week."* She was under nine years of age at the time and reaped with a scythe. She later became the village Post Mistress.

During the shooting season, many boys took days off to go as beaters for the Swakeleys shooting parties. For this they were paid a shilling a day and had for their lunch large slices of ham and beef between thick slices of bread, spread liberally with beef dripping. Few of them would have had such food but for the shoot.

"No school today on account of the preparations for Concert given by Miss Clarke for the benefit of the Church Organ." "William Clark has been absent without leave for a fortnight, his father kept him away to go hay-binding." "Charlotte Clayton absent helping her father." He, too, was a haybinder. This work is the cutting into trusses of the hay ricks. The trusses are held together with ropes of twisted hay. The making of these ropes is a double-handed job, usually undertaken by the haybinder and a lad. This craft was handed from father to son

Philanthropy and Education

for generations, so it is easy to see why the binder kept his lad from school.
"*Many children are away picking blackberries.*" "*John Batchelor had a fortnight leave*". As the eldest of six he could earn a few shillings at 'bird-scaring'. "*George Ford also scaring birds.*" This job was done for farmers who had sown fields of corn. The birds to be scared were rooks and pigeons. "*Sarah Ford was punished for hitting another girl.*" "*This morning Sarah Ford and her three brothers are absent as a protest.*" "*Fred Ford has been absent haymaking.*" "*Fred Ford is potato picking*". "*Aug 24th. 1898. Fred Ford has been absent from school for some weeks. He returned this week in an idle state, and has twice been threatened with punishment. This morning he had some apples taken from him, and at twelve o'clock he took them from the desk without my permission. For which I punished him this afternoon. He was very violent and abusive. I have therefore locked him in the porch for the afternoon....*"

Fred stayed at home for several days after that. Apparently he was a troublesome youngster, but he grew into a hard-working, steady-going man, softly spoken, with an air of aloofness about him.

When Beauchamp T. Pell, the rector's son, was home on holiday from his public school, he and his friends attended school occasionally to give some lessons. His name appears on the 1914-18 War Memorial tablet in St. Giles'.

Although the school was opened in 1873, the first mention of arithmetic in the log book was dated April 23rd, 1875. "*I have this week begun teaching the second class Compound Addition.*" The government inspector's report for the year ending 30th September, 1876, reads: "*The children are tidy and well-mannered but the attainments are sadly defective, especially in arithmetic. The infants are now comfortably housed in a small classroom but their instruction is almost entirely wanting. The children must be checked from their bad habit of copying.*" For the first time, Miss Anne Wilson is entered in the inspector's report as "*Cert. Teacher of 3rd Class with monitor.*"

In November, 1877, Miss Clarke called to give Certificates of Merit to Charlotte Bruce and Alfred Andrews, who passed in reading, writing and arithmetic. She also returned them their school pence for the year as a reward. This is the first mention of school fees being charged, and may be the reason why some of the pupils at Home Farm did not immediately go to the new school. Later references to money occur when a child is noted as leaving school to take up work, but "*owes a deal of school money.*" On occasions, pupils were fined for persistent absence. One entry reads: "*The acorns still seem to be the cause of children not attending school. I have seen the attendance officer, he says it is useless taking them to court as the Magistrates will not convict, and in cases where they do, the fine is so small, usually a shilling or one and six, that they do not mind.*"

The inspector's report of 1878 makes dismal reading: "*There is one good point in this school, the reading of the third and fourth upper girls, and the needlework is fair. Beyond this I cannot find anything satisfactory at any point, but I hope better things are in store for the school under a new teacher. My Lords will look for great improvements in this school if the unreduced grant is to be paid next year.*" Miss Wilson had resigned.

1879, Jan. 20th. "*The charge of Ickenham Village School given to Maude Gertrude Lowman, Certificated Mistress, trained in Whitelands Training College 1877-78 by Miss Clarke.*" This does not mean that Miss Clarke trained the new teacher, but that she gave her the appointment. "*Jessie Perkins on trial as Monitress probationary for Pupil Teacher, if successful at the approaching*

Ickenham Pond about the turn of the century

examination."

The inspector's report for 1881 was more depressing than the earlier ones and concludes: *"J. Perkins has passed an unsatisfactory examination. Should she be required to complete the staff and fail to the same extent next year, the Grant will have to be reduced."*

A somewhat cryptic entry reads: *"The lessons on Wednesday morning will be taken on Thursday afternoon."*

In those days, left-handed pupils were made to write with the other hand. Another entry in the Log reads: *"W. Prior left handed, a great drawback to the class."* (It was probably a greater hindrance to the teacher). A visiting school inspector once carried out an experiment into left-handedness. He had noticed that one of the boys in the top class suffered from a stutter. With the headmaster's permission, he asked five of the boys, including the one who stuttered, to cut a piece of paper. Each of them was to hold the scissors in his right hand. They all did that easily. Then they were told to repeat the exercise using the left hand. Only the boy who stuttered could do this. This convinced the inspector that it was wrong to force a left-handed person to write with the other hand.

During the 19th century and the early part of this one, the school was often closed for periods when children were admitted to the isolation hospital at Hillingdon suffering from scarlatina, scarlet fever, chicken pox, diphtheria and other contagious and infectious diseases. Sometimes as many as ten children were there at the same time. Not all came out alive. Two of one family died within a few days of each other. One girl died two days after admission. Teachers often visited the hospital to look through the windows at their sick pupils to give them encouragement. One master made a point of going twice each week.

The school was closed in September 1902 owing to an outbreak of scarlet fever. It opened again in October, but closed five days later because of another outbreak. During the closure, two of the best pupils, Percy French and Christina Gordon, died of the fever.

When the Great Western Railway was being constructed across the Green, the navvies engaged on the work lived with their families in huts nearby. Their children were taught at a dame's school. Little is known of this, but it is thought to have been held in one of the nearby farms and run by a farmer's kinswoman. The neighbouring farms were Copthall, Brackenbury, Gatemead and Beeton's Wood. The dame school did not last long and, on its closure, more than a dozen of the hut children were admitted to the village school. A few weeks later, the rumour spread that smallpox had broken out among the hut-dwellers. Villagers would not send their children to school unless the hut-dwellers were excluded. As most of the school managers were away on holiday, David Brickett, the remaining manager, agreed that the hut children should not attend. None of them went, anyway.

A month later, Dr. Clarke issued a medical certificate giving the navvy camp a clean bill of health. On receiving it, Mr. W. A. "Gaffer" Lee, the headmaster, gave it as his opinion that the outbreak could not have been smallpox or the results would have been more terrible. The hut children had a bad attendance record throughout. Some of the families settled in the village and their descendants are still here.

Apart from the days when children were playing hookey or when they were absent on the orders of their parents to earn money by acorning, blackberrying, bird-scaring and other jobs, there were a fair number of official holidays. Many were sad occasions to attend the funerals of well-loved people, such as David Brickett, the Rev. Pell and his wife, Thomas Truesdale Clarke, and Mr. Lee's wife, who had also taught at the school.

During the many epidemics, which people endured in those days of limited medical knowledge, the death rate was high, particularly among the young. In this respect, the rich suffered as much as the poor. Many half days were granted so that pupils could go to the funerals of their friends, or pay their last respects at the burial of a teacher, his wife or his child.

But there were more joyous occasions, when the hunt came to the village and the children followed the hounds. Other red letter days were the Queen's Jubilees, the Relief of Mafeking and Ladysmith, the end of the Boer War, Armistice Day, 1918, coronations and royal weddings. Once a visit was paid to the Zoological Gardens in Regent's Park. In the early days of the moving picture industry, several classes were marched into Uxbridge to see the new wonder of the age. The "Empire Electric" cinema had an elaborate name and facade but was known as "the Flea-pit". You could catch as good a flea there as you could at school. Holidays were given for cricket matches at Swakeleys, and on rare occasions at the Uxbridge cricket field. In one such match at Uxbridge, between Middlesex and Surrey, B. J. T. Bosanquet, the inventor of the 'googly', played for Middlesex.

It was in 1888 that it was recorded that every child on the school

The Story of Ickenham

books had attended that day.

"*1893 4th November. Miss Sybil Cochrane, grand-daughter of Clarke-Thornhill, promised some prizes to those children who attend most regularly from this week until the Christmas Holidays. The winter of this year was particularly severe, and on occasions it was thought fit to cancel school for as much as a week at a time on account of persistent bad weather.*"

"*1895 3rd April. Seven girls and three boys were punished this afternoon for continuing to play kissing games in the playground after being warned.*" The incident was mentioned to Mrs. Maude Jarvis, who celebrated her 94th birthday in September, 1978. She remembered it well, as she was one of the girls. Mrs. Jarvis was born in Ickenham and lived there all her life.

"*1897 17th May. The habit of spitting on slates must be vigorously put down.*" "*19th July. Priscilla Amer and Louisa Lucas, travelling children from the caravans on the Green, were admitted this morning.*" "*15th Sept. Alf ..... came to school very dirty. He has been spoken to several times about being dirty. He was washed by one of the older boys and has not been to school since.*" "*11th Oct. George ..... came to school in a filthy condition and was washed by Albert Montague in my presence.*"

"*18th Nov. Mr. Barrett has stopped the gamekeepers from employing school boys for beating.*" "*19th Nov. Notwithstanding the above order, Alfred Lawrence aged twelve and Bertie Stent aged seven are out with the shooting party today.*" Lady Maude Barrett's family were the tenants of Swakeleys at the time.

It was during the year 1898 that the labourers objected to their children being taken before the Magistrates' Court and fined for not attending school regularly. Their plea was that estate farmers kept their children from school to help on the farm, and no action was taken about that by the school managers. The continuing entries in the log book concerning absenteeism among the labourers' children indicate that the labourers believed that the law which governed the farmers' children also governed theirs.

"*1899 10th Feb. "The Stouts have gone into the Workhouse.*" "*17th Feb. The reason for Ernie Stout's name being taken off the books was because the family went into the Workhouse. But for some reason they have returned to the village.*"

"*28th Aug. "Sixpence of the Shoe Club money was missed from the Master's desk during playtime. The Master tried by every means in his power to get it restored but without success. As a last resource he had the shops watched after school* (there were only two shops). *When it was seen that Elsie ...... changed it, she was punished and shown how wrong it was*".

The following report was entered by Mr. William Halliwell, the headmaster, on the 18th of Sept. 1899. It concerned the school house which adjoined the school at the southern end. "*The back door cannot be bolted, through a defective bolt. Last evening after returning home from a walk, we found a man lying in the kitchen. A policeman was fetched. He searched the man, finding nothing suspicious. Everything in the house was safe, and, as the man appeared to have made a mistake through drink, I let him go.*"

The records show that until 1904 the necessary books, pencils and other equipment essential to a school seemed to be out of reach for one reason or another. But after that date, crayons, exercise books, reading books, plasticine, rubbers, chalks, slates, pens and rulers were more readily attainable.

Later that year, Ben Woodman of Ruislip, a popular boy, died suddenly of the croup. The children, accompanied by two teachers, attended his funeral at Ruislip, and took a floral harp for which they had all subscribed.

As soon as it became known under what appalling conditions our "Contemptible Little Army" was fighting in the early days of the 1914-1918 War, the girls of the school began knitting socks, scarves and other woolly garments for members of the forces. The Gilbey family at Swakeleys gave twenty-one pounds of wool to start the scheme, and the rector, Canon Bury, gave ten shillings. While the girls did the knitting, the boys devised various activities to raise funds to buy more wool. Fifteen pairs of socks were completed in the first six weeks of the War. This effort continued right up to the Armistice more than four years later.

As the War dragged on and food supplies began to be a problem because of the U-boat blockade, "Gaffer" decided to start a school garden. He prevailed upon his friend and fellow Parish Councillor, "Floppy" Cowne, to let him use part of his orchard, where the Public Library now stands. The girls would mark out the plots and the boys would do the digging.

One of the boys thought he saw a baby rabbit in a hole amongst the roots of the potatoes. He put his hand into the hole. A second later, he pulled it out with a full-grown rat dangling from his finger. The rat did not release its teeth until "Gaffer" ran it though with a fork. Then he and the boy biked into Uxbridge to have the finger cauterised by a doctor. A hard lesson was learned that day.

Though the school was a Church of England School, other denominations could still attend. However, each day always began with prayers led by the rector, the Reverend B. H. St. John Pell, and then a scripture lesson taken by the head teacher. When some Jewish children arrived as refugees from the air-raids, they were allowed to read books of their own choice during the scripture lesson. This did not please some of the Christians.

The weather figures in two entries in the log book. There was such a heavy snow on the night of 16th January, 1918, that only 22 children were able to get to school next day. They all lived close to the school. On April 8th, 1921, all the children were taken into the playground to watch an eclipse of the sun. Each of them had a piece of smoked glass to protect his or her eyes.

Two radio personalities visited the school. One was J. C. Stobart, the school inspector for January, 1920. He was the B.B.C. Education Adviser, but was chiefly known as the composer and reader of "The Grand Goodnight". This broadcast took place during the last hour of each year and mentioned every part of the Empire. Perhaps better known to the children was Cyril Hodges "Uncle Peter" of the B.B.C. He was also organist at St. Giles' and on January 18th, 1923, he and the rector, the Reverend D. W. Carmichael, with some of their friends, provided tea and entertainment for the schoolchildren.

The following entry in the school log book, made by Mr. Lee, and dated the 5th of October 1923, will be very gratifying to the family concerned: *"This week I have had to take off Horace, Winnie, Elsie and Violet Nash, who have gone to reside at Uxbridge. I am exceedingly sorry to lose them because of their good conduct and abilities."*

Tools for woodwork classes for the boys were obtained and brought into use in 1925. After praising the work and the results obtained by the teachers collectively, the inspector added the following paragraph: *"After many years' service in the village, the headmaster still takes the largest class himself, and manages the school quietly but effectively"*. Another teacher is praised in the entry for May 7th, 1926: *"Mrs. Slattery was unable to reach school in time on Tuesday the 4th owing to the General Strike. By alternately walking and cycling she reached school at dinner time, having covered the sixteen to twenty miles from Fulham."*

In 1928, over-crowding made it necessary for the older pupils at the Church School to move to the village hall, which was then referred to as Ickenham Temporary Council School. The next year, the old building was closed in preparation for the widening of Ickenham High Road. The older children were moved again, to a new building in Long Lane, whilst the infants took their turn at the village hall. Both schools were run by the County Council. In 1937, Breakspear Primary Junior and Infant School opened in Bushey Road. This school had 568 pupils in 1982.

The village hall period is remembered with affection by several of the old pupils, though the hall was very crowded. Three classes of young children were taught simultaneously, each group facing a different direction. The head teacher, Mrs. Slattery, was known as "The Governess". Anyone caught swearing by her would have his mouth washed out with soap.

But there was a jollier side to the village hall school. On Shrove Tuesday, pancakes were made in the tiny kitchen. (It was not extended till the War, when the hall was a British Restaurant.) At Easter, eggs were hidden around the stage and the children went hunting for them.

The next major change did not occur till 1952, when the boys from Ickenham County Council School in Long Lane were transferred to Abbotsfield County Secondary School in Hillingdon. Their old school became Swakeleys Secondary Modern Girls' School until 1973, when the girls moved to Clifton Gardens, Hillingdon. The former girls' school is now the North Hillingdon Adult Education Centre. The year 1952 also saw the founding of Glebe Primary Junior and Infant School off Glebe Lane. It had 204 pupils in 1982.

Douay Martyrs Secondary Modern Roman Catholic School in Long Lane was opened in 1962. It began with 450 pupils and today has 862. A much smaller private establishment, the High School for Girls, closed in 1964. It had been in existence since 1925 and, for all but the first two years, had occupied the Old Rectory.

Chapter Seven
Leisure and Pleasure

For much of the 19th century, Ickenham enjoyed two fairs, a cattle fair held on April 30th and a pleasure fair held usually in May or early June. By the early 20th century, there was just one fair, held on the Thursday before Whitsun, a week after Ruislip fair.

In those days, all the roads leading into the village had wide grass verges. Long Lane had swards on both sides, whilst Back Lane had only one. The verges of the Ruislip Road were so broad that the school and school house were built on them. These verges made ideal sites for the gypsies to camp with their caravans and horses before the fair.

According to the charter by which the fair was governed, the showmen could claim sites for their stalls by laying down poles. These sites could be claimed from noon on the day before the fair. At six o'clock, they were permitted to bring in their caravans, after which they were entitled to stay until nine on the morning of the day following the fair. The local policeman made sure that these rules were observed.

One year the time for pole-laying arrived but no policeman was to be seen. The gypsies seized the opportunity to drive in their caravans at once. When the policeman arrived an hour or two later, he told the showmen to harness up and "get out of it" until six o'clock. Most obeyed, but a few, unaware of the devastating qualities of this particular officer, raised objections. They all had to go. Soon there were only the poles left behind.

The policeman arranged with the gypsies that he would be at the pump at six o'clock in full view of the three approach roads. At the stroke of six (by his watch, not theirs!) he would drop a white handkerchief. As the time drew near, the gypsies jockeyed for position, completely blocking the three roads. Other road travellers had to wait. The villagers, especially the young – for the whole village had heard about it – took up vantage points, standing at front doors, at bedroom windows, on the churchyard wall, in farmyards and gardens, anywhere but on the roads.

On the stroke of six, the signal was given and, in the twinkling of an eye, the village was transformed by a mad, seemingly uncontrolled charge from three directions. In they thundered, horses galloping and caravans swerving and swaying until it seemed they must collide or turn over in the rush. But with the slightest touch on the reins the horses went the other way to restore the balance. In a matter of seconds the caravans were back in the positions they had occupied a few hours earlier.

Before the 1914-1918 war, the fair included sports and contests of all kinds. It was the village's big day. The prizes to be won were displayed on long lines stretching from the pump to 'The Coach and Horses' pub sign. There were dolls, all kinds of toys, shirts, dresses and other useful articles. The prizes had been given by the Squire's family, the Rector, farmers and others who could

The Story of Ickenham

afford to contribute. Apart from races and contests of strength and skill, there were two events which caused lots of laughs and amusement. These were the catching of a greasy pig for the women and straddling the greasy pole for the men. The pole was fixed horizontally across the deepest part of the pond and rested on a cart at each side. After each contestant had made his attempt to cross the pond, the pole was re-greased for the next man.

But it was the women's event which caused the most merriment. It often ended in uproar. The competing women gathered at one end of the village, and the greasy pig was released at the other end and driven towards them. The winner was the one who succeeded, not only in catching it but holding on to it as well. The grease made it difficult at first, but each time it was caught it lost a bit of grease and the task became progressively easier. Many an argument ensued as to which of half a dozen hands had caught it. One woman would have it by the ear, another by the tail. Which of the two had caught it? The Squire and the Rector were there; they had to be or civil war might have broken out. One or both of them adjudicated and, with many mutterings and under-breath swearings, that would be the end of it.

One year, even their brand of wisdom was sorely tried. The pig was eventually caught by a young married woman of gentle disposition. She had it fairly and firmly and it was well and truly caught. Up rushed the young woman's sister-in-law, as cantankerous a baggage as you might meet in a day's march. She grabbed hold of the now exhausted pig, and yelled to all and sundry that she had caught it.

The whole village knew she had not, and told her so, and then she exploded. The air was blue. To avoid a family split, which might have taken years to heal, the Rector talked with the gentle one. This dear soul agreed to share the prize. "Blessed are the meek for they shall lose half a pig."

Letters for the gypsies and show people would be sent to the village Post Office "to be called for". Some amusing scenes were then enacted as the travelling people slipped in to collect their mail from Miss Ellen Butler, Post Mistress from 1901 to 1939. The gypsies would come in as unobtrusively as possible, some of them almost furtively. None of the others must know they had received a letter. Having given the right name to Miss Butler, the letter would be handed over. The performance was always the same, only the players were different. A beautiful, swarthy young woman or a fine-featured, dusky young man, the play did not vary. The recipient would hold the treasured letter for a moment, then thrust it eagerly forward: "Read it for me, lady, would yer?"

Miss Butler would, and did. She read a letter to a girl who could not read, from a young fellow who could not write. The letter had been written by the postmistress of another village, or the wife or daughter of the postmaster. For if a man happened to be in the shop, whether serving or being served, the young lover, whether a girl or young man, would wait until only a female, no matter of what age, was in the shop.

After the letter had been read, the girl would tuck the precious epistle into her dress or blouse. "Would yer write a letter to 'im for me, lady? Go on, there's a dear, would yer?"

Again Miss Butler would and did: "Is there anything special you would like me to tell him?" she would ask. "Oh, y'know lady, tell 'im I loves 'im an' all that, an' tell 'im I'll try an' see 'im at Pinner." Then would follow a list of the fairs the girl's family were going to, and the address to which the next letter should

Leisure and Pleasure

Ickenham Post Office 1911, with Miss Ellen Butler in the doorway

be sent. The girl herself would seal the envelope, put the stamp on and post the letter. This always gave them a particular thrill; it made them a part of it. Anything up to half a dozen such letters were read and answered at each fair time. Such love-making by proxy was all part of the life of a village postmistress.

The old village post office was in a shop between Home Farm and 'The Coach and Horses'. Before Miss Butler, her father, Daniel, had run the post office from about 1890. C. S. "Charlie" Butler began the family tradition back in 1887. He was a baker as well as postmaster, and supplied corn to the local farmers. His shop sold everything from bacon, bred, killed and cured at home, to paraffin and snuff. Going further back, to 1878, the post office was in the care of a grocer, A. E. Ball, and before him it was J. Bryant, a corn dealer. Anne Montague's was the earliest recorded "receiving house" for post (1847).

Under the terms of the charter, Ickenham fair would only continue to be held so long as one stall-holder attended on the official day. One year, the right was almost forfeited. It happened that the Thursday before Whitsun fell on the 16th of May. That was the date of Hillingdon fair which, being much bigger, naturally attracted all the gypsies. None of them turned up at Ickenham. Groups of disappointed children drifted away to their homes. But the gypsy grape-vine worked so efficiently that a hoop-la stall at Hillingdon was dismantled late in the evening and rushed down Long Lane to Ickenham. The stall did very little business but that did not matter. The right to attend had been preserved.

Ickenham fair drew more people from outside the village if it was known that a big roundabout would be there. The roundabout always stood in the forecourt of 'The Coach and Horses', which would be cleared of carts and wagons awaiting repair at the smithy. The music of the organ could be heard far away and the occasional shrieks of the engine whistle advertised to all that a fair was being held.

The blacksmith, Llewellyn Wood, known as "Woody", had a young apprentice who took a great interest in the way the roundabout was designed. The young man, (who was the author's brother, Walter,) served as a smith in the artillery during the First World War. Injured and discharged from the army, Walter was no longer able to work as a smith. He turned his talents to constructing a replica of the roundabout which so fascinated him. He used only the simplest tools, a penknife, a fretsaw and various grades of sandpaper. His fourth model was a masterpiece. Electrically driven, its horses rose and fell seven times for every two revolutions. The roundabout was accompanied by vans, traction engines and caravans in authentic colours. Like the real thing, the model roundabout could be taken to pieces and packed away into the vans.

For many years, Ickenham was visited by the roundabout owned by Mrs. Pettigrove. She was the widow of Tom Pettigrove, a Romany if ever there was one. The old lady had her caravan so placed that she could count the passengers on each ride. With a son on each half of the roundabout, she knew how much money each of them should bring her before it had gone round twice. One year, she was so ill that she could not leave her bed. Nevertheless, the caravan still had to be in the right position for her to see. They still had to take her the correct amount before the ride ended. As the evening drew on, the crowds got bigger, the roundabout was always full and the rides got shorter. The big roundabout always added to the gaiety of the evening. Wally had made friends with the Pettigrove boys in the pre-war days. The friendship was renewed after the war. They were amazed at the wonderful model he had made of their family roundabout.

Finally, there came a year when no caravans arrived on the appointed day. It was the Wednesday before Whitsun and no gypsies had been seen. The children came hopefully out of school, but there was nothing for them to see. Even on fair day itself they did not give up, though they were hopeful rather than expectant. But nothing came. There was no fair in the district from which a stall could be sent, as had happened in the past. So in 1936 the right to hold a fair in the roads and village of Ickenham was lost for ever.

In those days before the First World War, the word "sport" meant huntin', shootin' and fishin', to the countryman. All the rest were games. Our village had its fair share of shooting, but there was no fishing in the parish. On a few occasions, a captive stag was brought to the village in an enclosed van, let loose, and then chased by the horsemen, dogs and people on foot. The stag could be hunted a dozen times. Given fair treatment, a stag will outrun any pack of dogs.

During the time allowed by law for the shooting of game birds, organised shoots were held by the owners or tenants of Swakeleys House. The responsibility for the smooth running of a shoot was in the hands of the head gamekeeper. It usually began and ended in one of the Home Covers, that is, close to the mansion. Other woods and spinneys were included so that there were several different routes which could be taken, but all started and finished near the House, so that the gentry had no unnecessary walking to do.

If there were not enough beaters to be had by the employment of casual labour, older boys from the school were given the day off to take part. For this they were fed and paid a shilling a day. Being boys, they would gladly have done it for the grub. Most shoots took place on a Friday, except at Christmas, when it was governed by the feast day itself. Another to which all the tenant farmers were invited was known as "the Farmers' Shoot."

Whatever the route taken, Gutteridge Wood was always included. It was the halfway stage. Lunch was always taken in Rough Field, adjoining the wood. Rough Field was a natural haunt of foxes, hares and plenty of other wild life. It was a stretch of rough grass and small thickets about twelve acres in extent, bordered on three sides by hawthorn hedges and meadowland and on the fourth by Gutteridge Wood. The entrance was a heavy wooden gate, and a little way into the field was a rustic log cabin. It was roofed with tightly bound faggots. Inside, there were seats along each side and a stout table down the middle. The "guns", as the shooters were known, has their lunch in the cabin. They were waited on by a footman who had arrived some time earlier to lay out the food and drink, which he had brought with him in a shooting brake. After the meal, he would take back whatever shot birds had been picked up.

The keepers, loaders and beaters ate their lunch seated on logs or tussocks. There was always plenty to drink and eat. There were thick slices of beef, ham and cheese between bread spread with rich beef dripping. Every beater took home more than he had eaten. There was beer for the men and ginger beer for the boys.

The estate had many woods and scrub covers, which were essential if there was to be a good supply of birds for the season. There were two hatcheries, one in a wide, grassy clearing in Gutteridge Wood, the other at the back of a long, narrow strip of woodland, known as Back Lane Cover. The site of the hatchery is now occupied by Thornhill Road. It was close to the River Pinn, then known as The Brook. The cover extended from there to Gospel Oak Cover. The oak tree is no longer there but a commemorative stone marks the spot where the tree once stood. The keepers kept a sharp look-out for pheasants' nests. They collected the eggs as soon as they had been laid, and put them under broody domestic hens in the hatchery. Sometimes, a pheasant would be allowed to hatch her own clutch if she was already sitting tightly when discovered. Keepers, however, like to have the birds bred under conditions where they can be adequately protected against foxes, weasels, stoats, and other predatory creatures.

In 1915, gamekeeper "Ducky" Stent, so-called because he waddled like a duck, was puzzled by something that was playing havoc with his birds around Gutteridge Wood. This area was Ducky's domain, and his experience told him that the mischief was being done by something he had not encountered before. Most predators leave certain traces which enable the keeper to know exactly what he's up against, but not this one. Ducky set a trap. The next day he found a golden eagle, caught by a leg but almost unhurt. It was taken to the courtyard at Swakeleys, where it was kept on a perch. A vet came in from Uxbridge to attend to its leg. When the bird was fit again, it was presented to the Zoological Gardens at Regent's Park by Mr. Arthur Gilbey, who resided at Swakeleys at that time. A brass plate on the eagle's cage recorded the circumstances of its capture and presentation.

Before the First World War, the people of Ickenham made their own entertainment. On one occasion, however, the Dawson brothers of Wood Lane, Ruislip, came to the schoolhouse with what they billed as a "lantern lecture" on

69

The Story of Ickenham

their travels in the Far East. The "lecture" turned out to be more of a friendly talk, and was received so enthusiastically that the Dawsons came again and again. In those days, there were no television documentaries for armchair travellers and a lantern show was a real attraction. After the Great War, the Reverend H. B. Langton continued these entertainments. He had lived in Egypt, and showed slides of the ancient monuments as well as scenes of contemporary life.

It was the Rev. Langton who formed Ickenham Debating Society. This group met in the large dining room of the old rectory, which later became Ickenham High School. This imposing building was demolished to make way for the Rectory Way housing estate in the mid 1960s.

Membership of the Debating Society was open to male parishioners over the age of fourteen years. It was agreed that women could not be admitted or there would be no point in the men going. The women already had the Mothers' Union and Mrs. Langton had introduced the Women's Institute. The debating rules were simple. Any subject could be debated as long as a proposer and opposer could be found. No one was allowed to interrupt these two, but when the speech for the opposition ended, the subject was open for discussion. The programme for each evening was decided at the end of the previous meeting. The Rector was inevitably the chairman of the society. No other member could have commanded the respect required to bring back to sanity some of the heated arguments which ensued.

On one occasion, a proposer was appointed for a subject but no one could be found to oppose it. The topic to be debated was "The Secret of Happiness". It was to be launched by Mr. Elliot. When all the pipes and cigarettes had been lit, the chairman called upon him to say his piece. Mr. Elliot thereupon told the meeting that he had decided to call his talk "What Makes a Man Happy?" In a very few words, he informed his listeners that the happiest man alive was "the tiller of the soil". As he was employed as a gardener to the Hon. Maude Lawrence at Ickenham Hall, he was well qualified to express that opinion. Although there was no opposer as such, a lively debate followed. From that day forth, Mr. Elliot was known throughout the village as "'Appy Man".

One of the more stormy members was Parish Councillor Cowne, who lived in a picturesque cottage where Ickenham Library now stands. It did not matter to him whether it was being proposed or opposed, when something was said with which he did not agree, he was on his feet to say so. One evening he made such an outburst that the chairman determined to put him in his place.

"Shut up, Cowne," said the chairman. "Floppy" Cowne (so-called because of his Flemish Giant kind of ears,) gulped and sat down. A few moments later, he was on his feet again, to interrupt the man who should not be interrupted. "Will you shut up, Cowne?" roared the chairman. "When he has finished, you can jaw to your heart's content, man. You're not at a parish meeting now." "Umph", grunted "Floppy" with a sheepish grin on his ruddy face. And so he learned the difference between a parish council meeting in the school and the procedure at a debate in the parson's dining room.

In those days before the First World War, the Men's Institute room in the High Road was a centre of social activities. Whist drives and social evenings were held on alternate weeks. For the rest of the time, the men of Ickenham gathered at the Institute room to play billiards, darts, dominoes and cards.

The men played a card game which, for want of a better name, shall be known hereafter as 'Ickenham Bridge'. The rules of this game were known to

Leisure and Pleasure

no one outside that room, and, if the truth be told, to few inside it, either. There were three great exponents of the game, Sam Saich, Reg Weeden and Harry Wilden. The fourth hand was played by anyone who would partner Sam. He had a favourite chair at this bridge table, and if, by chance or design, anyone was sitting in it when Sam came into the room, he would roam around like a lost soul until the offender got out of it. The game could not start without Sam, and he would not sit in any other chair. The tormentor had plenty of advice from the other two, and, if he knew what was good for him, he would get out of that chair.

   One of the calls in this brand of bridge was 'no bumper', which, being translated into English, was "no trumps". Whenever this call was made, no call could follow it, even if it was the first call. According to Ickenham rules, that was

*Orchard Cottage,
site of the present library*

The Story of Ickenham

it. This bid was often made by the player sitting in the fourth seat, usually for sheer devilment and to the annoyance of the other three.

A three-quarter-sized billiard table was in constant use by the younger members. It had long been the intention to acquire a full-sized table, but the room was not big enough. The decision was made to raise funds to build an extension. In 1913, a Grand Fete was held in Cowne's orchard. It was well organised by the secretary, Percy Catchpole, and it raised a good sum of money. The 1914-18 war put a stop to such schemes, but the threads were soon picked up afterwards.

The next gala day in the village was not for the making of money but for the spending of it in the spirit of joy and thankfulness. Peace celebrations were held in Buntings Field in 1919, when those who had been in the forces returned home again. Buntings Field is now part of Ivy House Road, where the Village Hall stands.

At a village meeting after the War, it was decided that everyone should take part in a drive to raise funds for the extension of the Institute room. As a tribute to those who had given their lives in the War, the new building would be called the Memorial Hall. Within two years, the Hall was built and a full-size billiard table installed. The Memorial Hall, a corrugated iron building, stood on the west side of Ickenham High Road until 1979, when it was demolished to make way for the Lynx House office building.

Mrs. Langton, the rector's wife, ran a Girls' Club in the Institute. There was a connecting door between the room where the girls met and the Men's Institute. This door proved too much of a temptation for the younger men. They would quietly unlock the door, push it open a little way and make eyes at any girl they could see. At this point, a young fellow might suddenly find himself shoved through the door into the room. The key would turn behind him. Taking a girl home after a dance was one thing, but facing a room full of them, with no means of escape, was quite another "jug o' tea". Only the "peeper" knew how he suffered, walking the length of that room with the girls giggling as he tried to apologise to Mrs. Langton. The girls seemed to enjoy the brief encounter so much that Mrs. Langton decided to allow the boys into the club for an hour's dancing at the end of the evening.

With the rise in the population consequent upon the development of the "Swakeleys" estate, the realisation came that a larger public hall was needed. Everyone now set about raising funds anew. Right from the start, it was agreed that the hall should be for the use of all, regardless of religion or politics. Everyone was encouraged to take out shares in the project at a non-repayable price of one shilling per share. Many took out more than one share.

The Village Hall in Swakeleys Road opened on January 8th, 1927. The architect, Clifton Davy, included a stage with dressing-rooms at the rear of the hall and a small kitchen at the side. During the Second World War, when the Village Hall was used by the government as a British Restaurant, larger kitchens were built along the western side of the hall.

As the population grew, the fields and open spaces for recreation became fewer. The meadow in which cattle grazed, now the Ivy House Road area, was known as the Cricket Field. The pitch itself was kept properly mowed, but the outfield was just as the cattle left it. No boundaries were marked. All hits were run, unless they landed in the next field on one side, or in Home Cover on the other. Home Cover was the piece of woodland between The Avenue and Ivy

Leisure and Pleasure

House Road.

There was no practice on Friday evenings. These were set aside for the preparation of the wicket. Nearly all local matches were played on similar grounds, which had been prepared by the players themselves under the same conditions. The Ickenham Club was well served by Percy Catchpole as secretary and Reg Weeden as captain. After the First War the Club carried on for a year or two on the same ground, but as development increased, the Club had to find a new home.

A part of the Rectory Field was fenced off. A new ground was drained and laid by Bill Druce and "Old Darky", a couple of casual labourers, under the supervision of the Cricket Committee, who probably knew no more about the job than the two old boys did. Be that as it may, they made a fair job of it. Reg Weeden continued as captain on the new ground, and the side was strengthened by the addition to the playing membership of the new Rector, the Rev. Langton. He had been a member of a winning crew in the Boat Race, but although a good cricketer, he didn't get a cricket blue. He was a slow bowler of no mean ability and on occasions represented the clergy.

He served the village club well until he exchanged livings with the Rev. D. W. W. Carmichael of Tenterden in Kent. Soon after his arrival, the Club moved to its present headquarters at the western end of Oak Avenue. The ground in the Rectory Field was taken over by a club which called itself "The Ickenham Exiles". The Rev. Carmichael had a certain sympathy with its members and joined them as a player. He was elected captain the next year and the club renamed itself "Ickenham St. Giles".

It was a change for the village to have in succession two rectors who were active sportsmen. Their predecessors were old men, the Rev. Pell, who died in harness, so to speak, and Canon Bury, who was 90 years old when he retired. Soon after the Canon retired to live in Kent, he was reading his newspaper when he came across his own obituary notice. The paper made amends the next day by publishing a picture of the Canon reading it. Several months later, after falling and injuring his leg, he read in the same paper a second notice of his death. Although over ninety years of age, he enjoyed the joke immensely. Remarking that he doubted if anyone ever before had read his own obituary twice, he said surely he should have been the first to know about it.

The rivalry between the villages of Ruislip and Ickenham was no less than in most rural districts. The sporting feeling was always high. This was particularly so at the turn of the century. Neither village could raise a soccer side, so they joined forces under the name "Kingsend United". Kingsend was a hamlet halfway between the two villages and consisted of half a dozen cottages, Kingsend Farm and the "White Bear" pub. In spite of this union, the team divided on one day each year to contend for the honour of each village. Not that the match was very honourable. In fact, it ranked almost as a blood sport. As soon as one team lost a player, it would try to bring down a member of the opposition. The match was a regular butchers' convention.

As many a man whose soccer days are over can still swing a bat, the villages found no difficulty in raising cricket sides. These played each other at home and away for many years until, with the growth of sprawling estates, the villages began to lose their identities.

The first tennis courts were in Buntings Field, where a self-service garage now stands. The council happened to be repairing the road nearby and the

The Story of Ickenham

steamroller driver was bribed to run his machine back and forth. The courts so created were rather rough and ready. The little bumps and dips caused the ball either to crawl along the ground or bounce head high. It was here that the Lavers and Lenglens of Ickenham learned the art of tennis.

The tennis players had to seek a new home when Griffith Evans bought the land on which the courts stood. Evans was a clever motor engineer. He bought an army lorry from the Slough dump, where there were hundreds of surplus vehicles from the Great War. He overhauled the lorry in a barn in Cowne's orchard and quickly sold it. After several more deals of this kind, he was able to buy the tennis court land and open a service garage. In the course of his work, he cut himself on a piece of copper and died soon after.

The tennis was resumed in Rectory Field, the site of the United Reformed Church. This home, too, was of short duration, and three courts were made in the shadow of the Rectory garden wall. A bowling green was prepared in the same part of the field. For a number of years, the Rectory Field was the home of all the outdoor sport of the village, the soccer club having their pitch behind the cricket pavilion. Eleanor Grove, Rectory Way, Charlton Close, part of Boniface Road and the present Rectory were all built on this field.

Swakeleys Road on the occasion of the 1908 Marathon

Leisure and Pleasure

When the Rev. Langton came to Ickenham, he so fell in love with the old church that he began a scheme which he called the St. Giles' Church Restoration Fund. Among his other efforts, he organised an "Olde Englishe Faire", which was held in the Rectory Field. Almost everyone gave a helping hand. Someone asked the Rector who would spend the money, if all the people were manning the stalls?

"We don't want our money," he said, "We want *their* money. I'm going to advertise this fair all around the area."

When our great day came, all the officials and helpers gathered early, dressed in clothes of a bygone age, weird top hats, frock coats, bustles and poke bonnets. All these were dragged out of attics and cupboards that hadn't seen the light of day for years. As buxom old Mother Dickens made her way to the field, top-hatted Jonesy was heard to remark, "I like yer bustle, ma." She gave her rump a resounding smack, and replied "That ain't no bustle, boy. That's me." The visiting crowds exceeded even the Rector's optimistic expectations, and the fair was a great financial success.

One of the main attractions at such fairs was the old-time skittle alley or nine pins. The prize was always a live animal, a lamb or a young pig, usually given by a farmer. Sometimes up to half a dozen players knocked all the pins down, so a time limit was set for a play-off to begin. This always created more excitement and was bound to attract folk for any such fair as might follow.

In the early 1930s, an argument ensued on a wet day in the cricket pavilion as to the pros and cons of promoting a sports meeting. Messrs. Harry Boyce, Bob Roberts and Spencer Squires accepted a challenge to back up their contention that, with the right approach, such an event could be held almost anywhere. They went into the project thoroughly and the sports meeting was widely advertised. Finchley Harriers, Thames Valley Harriers and Queen's Park Harriers sent athletes, including a relay team from each club. The standard of running was high, considering that the athletes were accustomed to running on cinders, not grass. The meeting was a financial success, too, the profit being devoted to the acquisition of a new cricket pavilion.

In the years preceding the First World War, the village had several outstanding athletes. Charley Winch, King Sims and Ernie Montague ran for the Polytechnic Harriers and Bert Taylor was an outstanding miler for the Finchley Harriers. At the annual athletic meeting held in the Ruislip Sports Field, these men ran against world class runners, including Willie Applegarth, the famous English sprinter.

The Olympic Games of 1908 were held in London. The course of the Marathon was from Windsor to White City, passing through Uxbridge and Ickenham. Many local people gathered to watch. The event was memorable because of the ill luck that befell the Italian runner, Dorando. He was the first man to enter the White City, but collapsed before reaching the finish and was helped to his feet by an over-enthusiastic fellow countryman. For this he was disqualified. Ickenham had its own marathon runner some thirty years later. He was George Nash, son of the landlord of 'The Soldier's Return', who competed several times in the Polytechnic Marathon.

Chapter Eight

Blacksmiths and Balloons

In the days before the motor car, the blacksmith played an important part in village life. Often one man performed the functions of blacksmith (who would undertake any work with iron) and farrier (whose speciality was shoeing horses). To fit a horse's shoes was a highly skilled job. The farrier was able to correct a horse's gait or enable it to cope with winter ice by roughening the shoes. During the 19th century, the blacksmith's traditional work of shoeing horses, putting iron tyres on carriages and carts, sharpening hand tools, such as bill hooks and scythes, and making pitchforks and plough coulters was enlarged by new developments. He was now required to undertake welding repairs on the early farming machines, the steam-or horse-thresher and later, the reaper. In the 1870's bicycle repair was added to his chores. Yet even so, the blacksmith often found it necessary to add another string to his bow. It was usual for a blacksmith to sell beer or coal or run some other small business besides the forge.

Before 1828, there was no full-time blacksmith in Ickenham. When a farmer had an employee capable of blacksmith's work, he would put the man at his neighbour's disposal. This sometimes caused friction. In 1828, several of the smaller farmers had decided that they were being charged too much and that the smith was not sufficiently available. On the 24th of June that year, a Court Baron was held to settle the grievance. Presiding over the court were the lord of the manor, George Robinson, his steward, James Banston, and the bailiff, Mark Haines. A piece of common land west of the Ruislip road was granted for the site of a smithy and cottage. The grant was proclaimed by Edward Browne, William Mayor, William Woodman and Thomas Byles for George Hilliard, a major landowner. At the regular court baron on October 20th, the grant was confirmed.

The first blacksmith's shop in Ickenham lay north of the entrance to the Green, by 'The Soldier's Return'. Forges were often established near a public house, where customers waiting for their horses to be shod could find refreshment. This particular tavern is said to have associations with Theodore Hook (1788-1841), wit and practical joker, who was educated at Harrow and is supposed to have gone on youthful binges in Ruislip and Ickenham. He was co-author of a comic opera called 'The Soldier's Return', which may explain the name of the inn.

In the early days, the Montague family ran the forge. *Robson's commercial directory...., 1838,* lists Ann Montague as both smith and farrier. This redoubtable lady was still running the "receiving house" (post office) and smithy whilst in her mid-sixties. Thomas Montague (died 1871) was blacksmith and landlord of 'The Fox and Geese'. In his time, the smithy was re-located in a lean-to attached to his public house. The old 'Fox and Geese' stood on a site in front of the present building, for in those days the Ruislip road was considerably

Facing: Ickenham Pond 1914, at left the 'Fox and Geese' and forge

narrower. The old hostelry was well-known for its rhyming sign:

> "Foxes on mischief are full-bent,
> Their nature is to tease,
> Their customers they do torment
> But mine I strive to please."

Thomas Montague was succeeded by William Montague, listed in the *Uxbridge Directory* as blacksmith until 1902. On retirement, he became the local road sweeper. A wheelbarrow tipped up, with the wheel in the air and the legs and handles resting on the ground makes a comfortable seat. A familiar sight along the village roads was the bottom of a barrow with a spiral of tobacco smoke rising from it, and Billy sitting snugly inside.

When the new landlord came into the ale-house, the smithy was taken over by a Welshman named Llewellyn Wood. He was a massive muscular man, who could ring the bell on the strength machine at the fair with either hand. After a disagreement with the pub landlord, "Woody" moved his scene of operations to the great barn at the back of the 'Coach and Horses' courtyard. At that time, the smithy at Eastcote was run by the Tappin brothers. The 'Fox and Geese' landlord prevailed upon one of them to use his forge. It was soon obvious that the village could not support two smithies, and Tappin went back to Eastcote to work with his brother.

The Story of Ickenham

The forge next to the 'Fox and Geese' about 1910

After getting well established in the smithy, for he was a fine craftsman, "Woody" opened a wheelwright shop under the same roof. The pub forecourt soon became full of carts and wagons in need of repair. Bert Brooks of Uxbridge was the wheelwright. Proof of the skills of these two master craftsmen was evident during a haymaking season early this century. A horse belonging to a farmer, who would ill afford to be without it at this busy time, was brought in to be shod. The horse's hoof was badly broken. Under normal conditions, the smith would not have done anything. But "Woody" knew the farmer's circumstances. He and Bert held a deep and wordy conference, and the two of them set to work. Bert spliced a bit of hardwood on to the hoof, making a cabinet maker's job of it, and Woody shod the half-wooden hoof. The result was as fine a piece of craftsmanship as you would see anywhere. The horse worked until the end of the haymaking season. The shoe and false hoof were then removed, and the horse turned out to grass until the hoof had grown again.

One of Woody's delights was to fire the anvil at village weddings. The anvil was taken to the middle of the pub forecourt and there placed upside down. Gunpowder was then poured into the exposed hole in the base. The firing device was a long length of iron dowel, which had already been heated in the fire of the forge. At the right moment, as the couple came down the pathway from the

Blacksmiths and Balloons

church, a touch of the powder from the red-hot tip of the iron, and they were greeted by a terrific bang which echoed all around the village. Every young couple expected it and none were disappointed.

Llew Wood carried on the business until circumstances forced him to transfer his smithy to a farm at Ruislip for the remaining years of his life. The village has since been without a blacksmith and forge. Even the spreading chestnut tree, beneath which the smithy at 'The Fox and Geese' once stood, has been felled in the interests of road widening.

'The Coach and Horses' inn played its part in the life and history of the village. The inn was built in the 17th century, and parts of the original building were in existence until recent alterations were carried out. The earliest documents concerning it are dated about 1759. The Court Baron, the institution for dealing with affairs of the manor, was often held at 'The Coach and Horses'. The homage, composed of the tenant farmers of the manor, sat with the lord of the manor or his bailiff and steward, meting out punishment to offenders. Some courts were held at the Manor House, but when Thomas Truesdale Clarke became the Lord of the Manor, he held his first Court Baron at the inn. The landlord of the inn at the time of the first World War was John T. Phillips, a Yeoman of the Guard.

If the smithy was of crucial importance to the farmers, the common or waste land was just as important to the farm labourers. On the waste they could grow vegetables, chiefly potatoes, and so supplement their meagre wages. The only other way was by poaching, but penalties against this were severe, including eviction of the poacher's family from their tied cottage.

In 1836, a court baron noted that "William Bunce and seven other

Ickenham village showing Llewellyn Wood's forge

THE VILLAGE INN & POST OFFICE ICKENHAM.

persons, being in receipt of parish relief, did dig up part of the waste land at Ickenham Green for gardens." They were still there the next year and the court ordered them to pay a shilling for each rood of land. (A rood = ¼ acre). In 1847, the names of these defiant gardeners were recorded in the Court rolls as follows: William Bunce, Abraham Andrews, Thomas Brill, Henry Bishop, James Finch, George Joel, Isaac Lawrence, Thomas Moss, John Neal, John Philip, James Bunce, Joseph Watson, Joseph Gregory, Joseph Norman, Samuel Taylor, Francis Wilden and Anne Weatherley.

The token charge mentioned above was paid for as long as the manor lasted. But when Uxbridge Urban District Council took over control of the parish in the 1920's, the allotment users refused to pay rent. There was no longer a lord of the manor and they had acquired deeds to their land under squatters' rights.

On the rest of the Green commoners had the right to graze their cattle. When grazing land was at a premium, owing to the farmers' anxiety to close as many fields as possible for the hay crop, it was used extensively. Cattle were turned out to grass and an old or disabled man earned a few shillings seeing that they did not stray, and bringing them back to the farm for milking at night. Villagers owning a pony or donkey hobbled it to keep it from straying. Hobbling was achieved by tying a strong soft rag into a rope around the lower forelegs. This would allow the animal to take short strides but it could easily be caught. The old Parish Council forbade the tethering of animals to trees or prepared stakes.

Owing to the value of the grass to ratepayers, gypsies were at all times unwelcome visitors. Around the turn of the century, they became more of a nuisance than hitherto. They arrived in larger numbers and stayed longer at the western end. The problem became so acute that the Parish Council and the Lord of the Manor circulated a declaration. It was read to those who were unable to read it for themselves. This was the declaration: *"We, the undersigned, being Occupiers and Ratepayers of Ickenham, do hereby and herein memorialize the Lord of the Manor of Ickenham, to assist in maintaining intact the rights of the Ratepayers to the use of the Green and in protection thereof from the now frequent use of the said Green by the Gypsies."*

Then followed the signatures of sixty parishioners beginning with that of Mrs. Louisa J. Cochrane, the widow of Admiral Cochrane, followed by some, but not all, of the farmers and most of the villagers. Those unable to write made a mark against their name, which had been written in for them. At that time, 1900, there were eighty-five householders in the parish. Some did not sign and gave the reason that their office forbade it. Others were probably afraid of the gypsies, but there was a good percentage of signatories.

The Marsh was another piece of land in which the villagers held Commoners' rights. It was a field and scrubland of fifteen acres at the most southerly end of Glebe Lane. A shooting brake road ran across it from north to south and then through several meadows to Rough Field and Gutteridge Wood. A small bridge of red brick carries the road over the Yeading Brook which passes from east to west across the Marsh.

This field of common land was for use by the villagers as grazing for their animals. Its use was governed by a list of bye-laws drawn up by the Parish Council. It was to be used from the first of May until the last day of September. During this time, a commoner could turn in one horse, one cow or two sheep. This simple rule, made for the benefit of all, was sometimes abused. A man with two ponies would claim that one belonged to his wife. One family of five had six head of cattle in the Marsh. The extra one was conveniently owned by a girl friend of one of the sons. There were no date regulations for grazing on the Green.

Until the beginning of this century, the shooting rights over the Green and Marsh were vested in the commoners. At a Parish Meeting held in the old school-room, a motion was put before those assembled that the Squire should be allowed to take over these rights. Two men only opposed this proposition. They were descendants of two of the allotment pioneers.

The following morning one of these men was ordered to quit his estate-owned cottage. A few days later, the other man was dismissed from his job on a farm, and ordered from his tied cottage. He was a good farm worker and had been on the same farm for many years. But the farmer for whom he worked was left in no doubt that his tenancy of the farm depended upon his worker's dismissal. Both men were soon accommodated at Ruislip, and found work there.

The last time a family was evicted under the tied cottage system was during the latter part of the First World War. The man and his young family were turned out, and their furniture stacked by the roadside at the mercy of the elements. A neighbouring farmer, Richard Keen, a kindly man of Milton Farm, heard of their plight, dared the wrath of his landlord and offered his help. The family had already been given shelter by villagers, so Farmer Keen had their furniture covered by a load sheet for the night. The next day, he had it stored in one of his barns until the man was able to find work and accommodation. The man's reputation as a farm hand was good, for he found work and a home a few days later in Hertfordshire.

A more pleasant incident happened one hot, sunny day in 1913. There was scarcely a breath of wind when a balloon was seen by some of the village children. It was drifting slowly from north to south and coming lower and lower. The children began to chase after it. They could see a man perched on the ring beneath the rigging. He was reading a book as casually as if he were in an armchair at home.

The chase continued along Glebe Lane. The children ran past the pond by the gate of Glebe Farm and across Manor Field. Some of them were quick enough to be at the orchard of Manor Farm just as the balloon landed. It came to earth in a shower of ripe fruit, which the children soon pocketed. The three balloonists were unhurt. They offered onlookers a ride but nobody was eager to accept.

John Pool, the farmer, and his wife invited the airmen to lunch. Afterwards, two of them resumed their flight. With a lighter load, the balloon rose rapidly. The children watched it for a long time, munching the apples now that they were out of Farmer Pool's sight. Hours later, the balloon could still be seen, hanging like a golden ball in the sky. It may seem a small thing in these days of space travel, but the landing of that balloon was quite an event to the villagers of 1913.

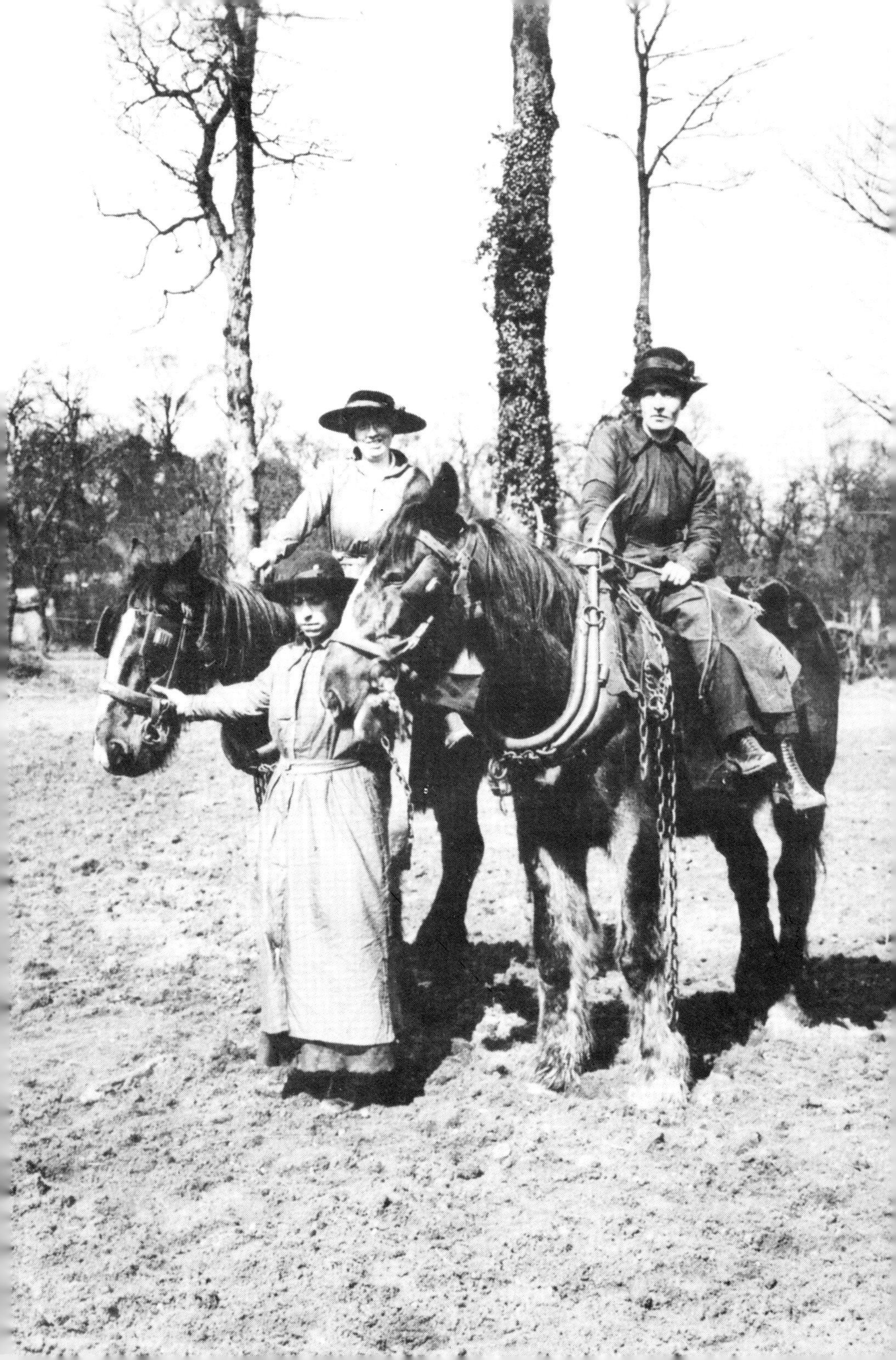

Chapter Nine
An Era of Change

The outbreak of war on the 4th of August, 1914, was brought home to everyone as first one man and then another was seen in a khaki uniform. Then they were missing from their usual haunts for weeks at a time, to re-appear when on leave from training. After a while, they were away from the village for much longer periods at the battle fronts.

The appearance of army officers in the district was an unwelcome sign that war was upon us. They came to every farm to commandeer the hayricks, leaving the farmer with only enough for his immediate bare needs. This did not please the farmers, for the surplus hay was normally trussed and transported to the stables of London business houses. It was therefore a part of the farmers' livelihood. Hay was as important then as petrol is today. The hay was baled by the Pioneer Corps and taken away to cavalry depots.

As the war dragged on its seemingly endless course, one sometimes saw a man in khaki making his weary way from the station. He would be unshaven, probably lousy, dirty, loaded with equipment, the mud of the trenches on his uniform, yet still able to raise a smile at the sight of a familiar face. "Ginger" King came home like that one day. He called at the house of Mrs. Hughes, a few yards from his own home, to tell her that he had seen her son going into action as he was coming out.

This was one of the stories told to the children of the school by Mr. W. A. Lee, the headmaster. Each morning they sat enthralled, as after the scripture lesson he told them of the war and its effect on the village. Sometimes his voice trembled with emotion, sometimes it was vibrant with pride. For he had taught them all, young and old alike; they were his friends. "Gaffer" was that kind of man.

Some of the stories he told were of heroism, some of misfortune and sadness. One day he told of Able-Seaman Joe Dickens, whose home was one of those squalid dwellings near 'The Soldier's Return', where he lived with his parents and young brother. Joe was already in the Navy when the war began. He was serving aboard the destroyer H.M.S. *Aboukir*. On Sept. 22nd, 1914, she was torpedoed in the North Sea by a German U-boat, and sank almost immediately. Joe found himself swimming for his life in the icy waters. At length he was picked up, when almost exhausted, by H.M.S. *Hogue*, a sister ship of the *Aboukir*. After a meal, and wearing warm, dry clothes, he felt like a new man.

He had not enjoyed this state of well-being for long when the *Hogue* was hit by another torpedo. She, too, sank quickly. Once again Joe found himself in the bitterly cold waters of the North Sea. Again the sea was cheated of its prey, for Joe was rescued by H.M.S. *Cressy*, a sister ship of the other two destroyers.

Once more he was fed and clothed by his rescuers. Then the *Cressy*

Facing: Ladies' plough team during the First World War

The Story of Ickenham

became the victim of the same fate as had befallen the other two ships. For the third time, Joe had to swim for his life. This time, he was fortunate enough to be able to cling to a piece of wreckage floating with him in the rough sea. After many hours, he was seen by the look-out of a homeward bound fishing trawler. He was in a pitiful state of exhaustion when taken aboard. Had it not been for the piece of wreckage, Joe would have drowned long before. His rescuers soon had him on dry land and he was rushed to hospital.

This was the story Mr. Lee told his pupils that sad morning. Unfortunately, it does not have a happy ending. Joe Dickens died several months later from the effects of his ordeal. He was one of 1,400 seamen who died when the three destroyers were sunk by the *U9*. The story can be found in Geoffrey Bennett's *Naval battles of the First World War* (1968).

Another story of heroism has nothing to do with active service but is, nevertheless, an epic. Soon after the creation of the Royal Flying Corps, later to become the Royal Air Force, an airfield was established on the fields of Down Barns Farm, Northolt, Glebe Farm, Ruislip, and Hill Farm, Ickenham. This was to become Northolt Airport and took most of the meadow and grazing land of Hill Farm. Depots for the new service were built in various parts of the country. Number Four Stores Depot was built at Ickenham on the pasture land of Home Farm. The site was bounded by the road to Ruislip, Austin Lane and the two railway lines.

Transport for the building project was carried out by traction engine and horse and cart. The horses were kept in a stable south of the Great Western Railway line. The stable was a wooden building with a tarred felt roof, the kind that would burn rapidly if it caught fire.

One warm summer evening, after the horses had been fed and bedded down, the night watchman saw something like smoke rising in the still air. He made a search and found that a fire had started in the stables. By the time he had 'phoned the fire brigade, the flames had spread alarmingly.

Mr. Lewis, the station-master at Ruislip and Ickenham Great Western Railway station, heard the screams of the terrified horses. He ran into the blazing stable and freed every horse he could reach. The intense heat finally drove him back.

Some troops of the U.S. Army happened to be camped on the north side of the railway. Seeing the flames, they seized the coil of fire hose kept on the railway platform, connected it to the hydrant and ran across the line. Before the water could be turned on, a London-bound express came up the line. The hose was cut in two.

The horses freed by Mr. Lewis were caught and taken to Church Farm, where a veterinary surgeon examined them next day. Some were so badly burned that they had to be destroyed immediately. None would have survived if it had not been for Mr. Lewis. He was a small man, quiet and reserved, but a giant in courage.

Another anecdote of the First World War concerns H. N. Southwell, Dame Nellie Melba's Australian concert manager. When war broke out, he was on board the German liner *Emden* en route to England. Finding himself in this country for longer than he expected, Southwell became war correspondent for two Australian newspapers. He stayed with a family in Ickenham.

Southwell went to France and Belgium several times to meet Australian troops on active service. He brought back many souvenirs. One of

An Era of Change

which he was particularly proud was a shiny brass object. He put it on the mantelshelf above the fire. It stood there for weeks, the good lady of the house keeping it polished.

One day, a son of the house came home on leave from France. He looked at the new ornament in amazement. "That's a Jerry aerial bomb," he said. "And a live one at that."

That night, he and Southwell took the bomb to Swakeleys. They rowed out on to the lake and dropped the bomb in the deepest water they could find.

This story has a sequel. After the war, Uxbridge Volunteer Fire Brigade used to come to Swakeleys lake to practise their drill. One day the nozzle of a hose blew off and sank in the lake. Next evening, the firemen dredged for the nozzle with long-handled rakes. But the muddy brass object they recovered was not the nozzle. An officer of the Royal Engineers was called. He told the firemen that what they had found was a German bomb, obviously dropped by a Zeppelin. He rendered it harmless and it was carted away.

One day Mr. Lee had sad news to tell the children. Arthur Winch, better known to everyone as Punch, was reported missing, believed killed. Arthur was yet another of his old pupils. The Winch family lived in a cottage opposite to the school. The parents had died long before and some of the children had married. Those still at home were cared for by a maiden aunt. She was a saintly soul, who could walk only with the aid of two sticks, and even then only with great difficulty. She was known throughout the village, to old and young alike, as Aunt Polly. The children vied with one another to do her errands. She was carried to her bed each night by one or other of her strong young nephews. If they were not available, there was always someone to help her.

The news about Punch kept the smile from her face for many days. The notice of regret arrived in due course from the War Office, and another well-known figure vanished from the village scene. It seemed strange that one morning, as Mr. Lee approached the school on his bicycle, Aunt Polly should be at her gate waving her stick in the air, the broadest of smiles on her ruddy face. "Arthur's all right", she called. "He's all right".

Aunt Polly and Gaffer were the only ones in the place who referred to Punch by his proper name.

Gaffer got off his bike, leaned it against the school fence, and asked the old lady all about it. She delightedly showed him the letter. He nearly danced with joy when he knew Aunt Polly had not "gone a bit funny".

A shell had buried Punch and his mates in the dugout. The uninjured had tried unsuccessfully to dig their way out. Many days later, another shell had burst in the same place and re-opened the dugout. All were injured by one or other of the shells. Punch had a fractured skull. The survivors were taken to base hospital, and then back to England. There was enough food left to have lasted the buried men for another week.

After some relieved and lighthearted chatter with Aunt Polly, Mr. Lee walked over to the school with a new spring in his stride. He rang the bell for school nearly half an hour late, but who cared? Punch had been amazingly lucky. Ken Weeden, who lived two doors from Punch, was killed in action on the day he arrived at the front line.

During the latter part of the war, it was not an unusual sight to see a schoolboy driving a pony and trap in which were two or three German prisoners of

85

The Story of Ickenham

war. These men were hired out to local farmers to help with the haymaking and other farm tasks. The prisoners were made conspicuous by large, round patches of a colour quite different from the rest of their uniforms. They were accommodated in a large house at Eastcote, and in another at the Denham end of Uxbridge High Street. The farmer was responsible for the transport of the men, but was ordered not to feed them during the day. It is needless to record that no farmer expects to get a day's work from an unfed worker, whether it be man or horse.

One bright Saturday morning, staccato sounds were heard and small white clouds suddenly appeared in an otherwise clear sky. The villagers looked towards London to see in the distance a number of aeroplanes flying back and forth. The viewers were Woody the blacksmith, an old man, some boys and a woman. "Germans", someone murmured fearfully. "Gun practice," said Woody hopefully. The black-looking planes finally turned to disappear in the haze of distance, and the guns stopped firing. "All those German princes have ended in smoke," said Woody.

That was the first daylight raid made by the Germans on the City of London. It became known as "The Saturday Morning Raid." Bombs were dropped in St. John's Wood Road at the entrance to Lord's Cricket Ground. But the worst damage was done at the printing works of Odham's Press, where many working girls were killed. The war had suddenly come closer.

From 1908 until the end of the war, the Rector was the Rev. William Bury, Canon of Peterborough Cathedral. He often took morning prayers at the Church School. He did this on the 11th of November in 1918. He then left the school and was back again a few hours later, bringing the news that an armistice had just been signed. The fighting and killing was at an end. "Off you go," he said, his grand old voice trembling with emotion. "Go straight home and tell your mothers the good news. No more school!"

The children soon went home to tell the news, but the measured beat of a drum brought them out again. The Americans camped by the Great Western station had organised themselves into a percussion band with almost anything that would make a noise and were marching toward the village. Kids came from everywhere and fell in behind them. Up Back Lane they paraded, into Park Road and across Uxbridge Common into the town, to meet another lot coming from Hillingdon House. They returned to Ickenham late in the afternoon. No one had eaten but they did not notice. Had it been a sponsored walk, those kids would have earned a fortune.

When they got back to the village, people were standing around in groups just talking. They had come in from outlying farms and cottages, drawn by a common desire, to talk, to belong, as though drawn by a gigantic magnet. The War had seemed so aimless. Every one was thankful beyond words.

Then old Harry Wilden began to dance. The effort almost made him fall over. "We must 'ave a bonfire then," he cried in his tremulous old voice.

He picked up two or three bits of paper and put a match to them. Old Billy Montague added some cigarette packets he hadn't swept up. Children scurried around to find anything that would burn. Nance Wiskin brought some empty sweet boxes. Sam Saich came up with a couple of faggots from his stack. Tom Randell brought two more. In a matter of minutes, fuel for the fire was coming in from all directions. Anyone who had anything to burn took the opportunity to get rid of it. Showers of sparks and flames shot upwards into the blackness of the night as each new contribution was hurled into the flames.

A red glow appeared in the sky toward Ruislip, another in the direction of Hillingdon, then Harefield and then Northolt, until quite soon the sky was alight with bonfires in every direction. Fires of happiness and relief. Old and young danced around them until they were tired out. Even then, no one seemed to want to go home; there were no thoughts of drink, either. Late that night, someone suggested that if they didn't go home to their beds, they'd all fall asleep standing up. The ashes of that fire were hot for days after.

With the beginning of the 20th century, a transport revolution came to Ickenham. The Great Western and Great Central Railways opened a line which passed through Ickenham on its way from London to the north and west. Before this, excursions to Ascot or the Derby and other annual trips were made in brakes drawn by two or more horses. To reach more distant parts of the country, travellers had first to reach one of the London termini. There was a G.W.R. station in Uxbridge from 1856, though it was not linked directly to London. The line went from Uxbridge to West Drayton and from there to Paddington or the west.

In 1900, the Joint Committee of the two railways acquired land from the lord of the manor, Randolph Clarke-Thornhill. Part of this land was a strip which would divide Ickenham Green into two parts. To compensate the commoners of the Green for this loss, they were given a field to the north west of Mad Field Cover adjoining the Green. More recently, it has been used for football and cricket pitches.

On 20th November, 1905, the Great Central and Great Western Railways opened their line through what is now West Ruislip. The station did not open till 2nd April, 1906. Where the railway passed over the River Pinn, a bridge and small road were provided alongside the stream, so that the commoners would have access to the part of the Green north of the railway.

The advent of the Metropolitan line, running almost at right angles to the Great Western, gave hope for even better travelling facilities. However, there were to be delays. Ickenham was not at first considered important enough to merit a station.

On the 30th of June, 1904, a special train left Harrow on the Hill to make the ceremonial opening trip to Uxbridge. The train consisted of an "E" class engine and five straight-sided coaches. The locomotive was bedecked with flags and a laurel wreath covered the smoke-box. As the train passed, villagers waved from the bridges in Austin Lane and Glebe Lane.

By March, 1905, the steam trains that had inaugurated the line had given way to electric engines and there was a service between Uxbridge and Baker Street. On the 25th of that month, Ickenham Parish Council passed a resolution asking Uxbridge Rural District Council to approach the Metropolitan Railway about a halt at Ickenham. This request is said to have made an Uxbridge councillor exclaim "What! A halt out in the wilds of Ickenham!" Nevertheless, the halt was built.

Opened on September 25th, 1905, the Halt was a modest structure of $8' \times 2'$ planks supported by joists mounted on concrete blocks. There was no room for more than three carriages at a time. Longer trains stopped twice. The platforms were not extended till 1922. The absence of any shelter for waiting passengers bothered the Parish Council, who requested such shelters in December, 1905. For many years, indeed until 1971, travellers had to queue for

The Story of Ickenham

their tickets in Glebe Avenue. So muddy was the road in the early days that staff at the booking-hut got used to looking after the wellington boots of commuters. These would be claimed for the dirty walk home.

The first booking-hut was built in 1910. As an advertisement, it flew a red flag, but this had unforeseen consequences. One windy day, the flag frightened a horse being led past the station. The man leading the animal was knocked over. The Metropolitan Railway lost the law-suit which followed, and the flag had to come down.

In those days, Ickenham was still a picturesque village. Visitors were charmed by the view of the little church surrounded by trees, as they turned into Long Lane from the station. There were few horseless carriages to dodge in those days. The railway brought many trippers from London, especially at holiday times, when six and eight coach trains were laid on. The villagers were quick to profit by all this. Tea shops opened. Bunches of flowers were sold at fourpence, fivepence, even sixpence. Only the farmers were unhappy; they had to put up notices to keep the townspeople from trampling their fields.

Until the coming of the Metropolitan Railway, the village's centre had been at the intersection of Back Lane (Swakeleys Road) with Long Lane and the Ruislip Road. St. Giles' Church, 'The Coach and Horses', the village shop and post office, the pond and Home Farm were all close to this intersection. But

An Era of Change

Panoramic view of Ickenham, 1913

the railway changed all this. As soon as it became possible to reach central London in less than an hour, Ickenham became a potential rural haven for commuters. Once land became available, as it did after the sale of the Swakeleys estate in 1922, new houses began to rise in increasing numbers. By the mid-thirties, the shape of Ickenham had altered radically.

Shops were built on the south side of Swakeleys Road and houses on both sides as far as the parish boundary. More houses and flats appeared near Swakeleys and beside Long Lane. Milton Farm, with its pond and listed barn, was demolished in 1939, during the development of "Ickenham garden city", the promoters' name for Milton Court.

Road widening and road building went on apace. The A40 Western Avenue was being built as far as the end of Swakeleys Road but was not completed until after the Second World War. Elms were felled along Swakeleys Road and Long Lane. The High Road was widened in 1935, necessitating the destruction of the old school and the original 'Fox and Geese''. By 1937, Swakeleys Road had become a dual carriageway. Three new residential roads now led off Ickenham High Road and more houses had risen at the east end of Glebe Avenue and on the south side of Austin Lane. Population figures give an idea of the rate of growth, though exact comparisons are impossible because the boundaries of the civil parish were enlarged in 1929. The population of the civil

89

The Story of Ickenham

parish was 443 in 1921 and 1,741 in 1931.

Ickenham had been caught up in the Metroland boom. The term "Metroland", first used in 1915, refers both to a dream fostered by advertising men and to the annual property guide of that name published by Metropolitan Railways Country Estates Ltd. The dream was of rural peace, "a Mecca to the City man pining for country and pure air". More prosaically, Metroland offered a frequent train service to London, low price season tickets, "excellent educational facilities", and golf courses "both numerous and good." The middle classes came to Metroland to buy houses; the working class came on day trips.

After the Second World War, building continued. Church Farm, opposite St. Giles', was demolished to make way for more shops. New houses went up along Breakspear Road South, Edinburgh Drive and Woodstock Drive. In 1957, a relic of the rural past, the ford over the Pinn, was replaced by a bridge suitable for cars. For twenty-five years after the war, there was continued growth in population and traffic. In 1951, the population of Ickenham was 7,107, but ten years later it had reached 10,370 and in 1971 it was 11,214. Then came a decline to the 1981 figure of 10,608. Probably this downward trend will not continue. A new housing estate called Brackenbury Village is being built on the site of the old West

Map of Ickenham in 1983

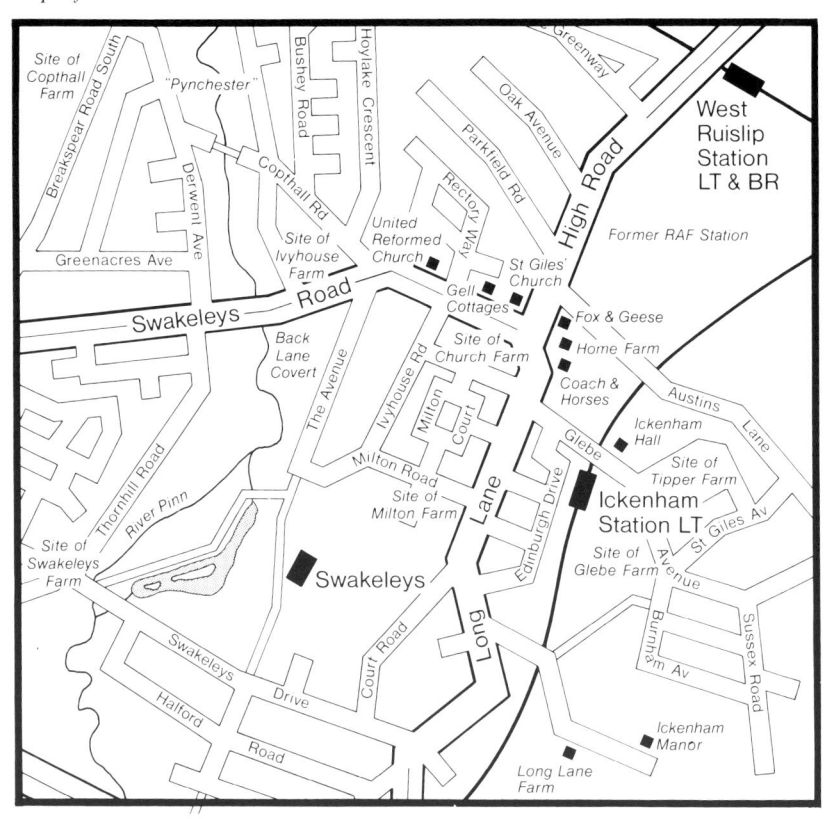

An Era of Change

Building on Swakeleys Road in the 1930's

Ruislip Air Base, used by the USAF from 1955. This estate will house perhaps 1,500 people. Other new houses and flats are to be built on Pepys Close.

The junction of Swakeleys Road, Long Lane and the High Road, once the centre of the old village, is now a focus for motor traffic. The latest attempt to control the flow was an experimental mini-roundabout, adopted in March, 1983. This typical feature of contemporary, car-orientated society stood just a few yards from St. Giles' Church, which has witnessed so many changes over the last six hundred years.

READING LIST

Books

EDWARDS, Dennis F. and PIGRAM, Ron.
  Metro Memories (1977).
  The Romance of Metroland (1979).
GODFREY, Walter H. Swakeleys, Ickenham (1933) *The standard work.*
JARVIS, L. Donald Free Church History of Uxbridge (1953) — *see Chapter X for Ickenham.*
VICTORIA COUNTY HISTORY OF MIDDLESEX Vol. IV (1971) pp. 100-109. *The chapter on Ickenham is by H. P. F. King.*

Leaflets

Many of these publications are out of print, but copies may be seen at the Local Studies Department of Uxbridge Library.

DAVIS, Jean
  The case of the pretended marriage (1976)
  Refers to Sir Robert Vyner of Swakeleys.
EDWARDS, Dennis
  Ickenham, a history in brief (1974).
  Swakeleys, a history in brief (1975).
  Ickenham, a walk around the conservation area (1976).
  Bygone Ickenham in pictures (1977).
  Ickenham country trail (1982).
  Yesterday in Ickenham (1983).
  — *Ickenham Residents Association publications.*
KINGSTON, P. D. A short history of the parish and church of St. Giles', Ickenham (1963).
ROQUES, V. J. A visitor's guide to Swakeleys (c.1960).
WATKINS, Bernard A history of the parish and church of St. Giles' (c.1935).
WILLIAMS, Brian Ickenham History Trail (Hillingdon Borough Libraries 1982).

Other Materials

The parish registers for St. Giles Church are kept at the Greater London Record Office, 40 Northampton Road, Clerkenwell, E.C.1. The old logbooks of Ickenham School are kept by the Rector of St. Giles'. Microfilm copies of the Census for Ickenham for the years 1841, 1851, 1861, 1871 and 1881 may be consulted at Uxbridge Library. Microfilm copies of local newspapers back to 1854 are also kept at Uxbridge Library.

INDEX

Page numbers in **bold** type refer to illustrations

Abbotsfield School 64
Aboukir, H.M.S. 83
Ackroyd, J. R. 42
acorns 58, 59
Acton, Sir William 19
Addison, John 40
Adkince, Ales 38
adult education 64
Aelmar 10
Affelde, Reginald 43
air raids 86
Allen, Araall 39
almshouses 52-54, **53**
Altam, Mr. 19
Alwin 10
Andrews, Abraham 80
Andrews, Alfred 59
Ansgar, the constable 10
Applegarth, Willie 75

archaeology 9-10; Gerrards Cross 9; Harefield 9-10; Heathrow 9; Ickenham 9; Pynchester 24
athletics 75
Atlee, James 37
Attelee, William 46
Austin Lane 84, 89
Avenue, The 23, 27

Back Lane *see* Swakeleys Road
Ball, A. E. 67
Banston, James 76
Barrett, Lady Maude 62
Barrow, G. F. 42
Bastwick, George 39
Batchelor, John 59
Battersby, Leonard 39
Battey, John 39

Beaureper, Hants. 18
Beauties of England, quoted, 38
Beckett, Oliver 18
Beckwith, Miles 39
Beetonswood Farm 46, 61
Bencraft, Henrietta 19
Bennett, Geoffrey: *Naval Battles of the First World War* (1968) 84
Bennier, Peter 26
Bingley, John 19, 23
birdscaring 59
Bird, William 13, 39
Bishop, Henry 80
blacksmiths 76-79, **77**, **78**, **79**
Blackwell, Francis 45
Blencowe, Mary 13
Blencowe, Thomas 13
Boniface Road 74

92

Bosanquet, B. J. T. 61
Boulter, R. 42
Bourchier, Sir Thomas 17
Boyce, Harry 75
Bracken, Thomas 40
Brackenbury, manor of 24
Brackenbury Farm 61
Brackenbury, Thomas 24
Brackenbury village 90
Bradeley, John 39
Breakspear House 10
Breakspear Road 90
Breakspear School 64
Brickett, David 41, 46, 61
Brickett, William 40-41
Brill, Thomas 80
British Restaurant 64, 72
Brocas, Bernard 18, 43
Brocas, Sir Pexall 18, 19
Brock, John de 13
Brock, William de 13
Bromley, Robert 19
Brooks, Bert 78
Brothampton, John de 39
Brown, Edward 41, 76
Brown, Nich. 39
Bruce, Charlotte 59
Bryant, J. 67
Brydges, Anthony 18
Bunce, Herbert 34
Bunce, James 80
Bunce, William 80
Buntings, The **33**, 52, 54, **89**
Buntings Field 72, 73
Burr, Eliza Woodyear 35
Bury, Rev. William 40, 63, 73, 86
Butler, C. S. "Charlie" 67
Butler, Daniel 67
Butler, Ellen 58, 66-67, **67**
Butler, Walter 58
Byles, Thomas 76

Caratacus 10
Carmichael, Rev. Douglas W. W. 40, 63, 73
Carnarvon, Lord 54
Carter, Howard 54
Cassingham, A. O. 42
Catchpole, Percy 72, 73
Catherine (Parr), Queen of England 38
Catuvellauni 10
Cemkine, Joanna 38
Charles I 19, 47; bust of at Swakeleys 20, 26
Charles II 19, 20
Charlton, Anne 17
Charlton, John 13, 17
Charlton, Sir John de 17
Charlton, Thomas de 17, 24
Charlton Close 74
Child, Richard 39
Chunky *see* Woodley, Philip
Church Farm 46, 84, 90
Churches *see* St. Giles' Church, Ickenham; St. Margarets' Church, Uxbridge; United Reformed Church
cinema 61
Clark, William 58
Clarke, Dr. 61
Clarke, George Hawkins 33

Clarke, Helen 32
Clarke, John Cholmeley 33
Clarke, John George 32
Clarke, Thomas 13, 14, 32-33, 38, 39, 40, 57
Clarke, Thomas Truesdale 14, 16, 33, 39, 57, 61
Clarke, William Capel 14-15
Clayton family 41
Clayton, Charlotte 58
Clayton, Henry T. 34
Clayton, Robert 36-37, **36**
Cleere, Andrew 38, 39
Clerkenwell Prison 48
Clinton, Henry 38
Clench, John 39
Coach and Horses Inn, 14, 43, **44**, 65, 67, 68, 77, 79, **79**, 88
Cochrane, Admiral Sir Arthur 54
Cochrane, Helen 30, 54
Cochrane, Louisa J. 80
Cochrane, Sybil 62
Collins, "Ike" 42
Colne, River 9
Colt, John 25
Colt, Maximilian 25
common land 79-81
Compass Community Arts Centre 35
constables 43, 46
Copthall Farm 15, 61
Cornish, William 39
Cotgrave, Eleanor 18
Cotton, Francis 18
Court Baron 43-46, 76, 79
Courtenay, Sir Henry 17
courts, manorial 14, 19, 43-46
Cowley, manor of 17
Cowne, "Floppy" 63, 70
Crab, Roger 47-49, **48**
Cragg, William 19, 23, 45
Crespigny, Sir Claude Champion de 54
Cressy, H.M.S. 83
cricket 61, 72-73
croquet 22
Crosyer, Robert 43
Cruickshank's Lodge 28
Crutcher, Richard 36, 37
Cunobelinus 10

Dabney, Dority 38
Davy, Clifton 72
Dawson brothers 69-70
Dearman, Henry 40
Derby, Earl of 45
Derwent, James 39
Devon, Earl of *see* Courtenay, Sir Henry
Dickens, Joseph 34, 83-84
disease 60-61
Domesday Book 12-13
Douay Martyrs Roman Catholic School 16, 64
Douglas, Lady Margaret 38
dovehouse 28
"Dum-dum" *see* Kendall, John
Dyer, John 39

earthworks, archaeology 9
Edinburgh Drive 90

Edmondes, Thomas 38
education *see* Schools
Edward, the confessor 10
Edward VII 41
Eleanor Grove 74
Elliot, Mr. 70
Elthorne Hundred 11, 14, 43, 46
Empire Electric Cinema 61
Esdaile, Katherine A: *English church monuments 1510-1840*, quoted 36
Essex, Earl of: a bust of at Swakeleys 20, 26, 34
Evans, Frederick J. 40
Evans, Griffith 74
evictions 81

Fafiton, Robert 13
Fairfax, Lord: bust of at Swakeleys 20, 26
fairs: Hillingdon 67; Ickenham 58, 65-68; Uxbridge 57-58
farms *see* Beetonswood; Brackenbury; Church; Copthall; Glebe; Hercies; Hill; Home; Ivy House; Long Lane; Manor; Milton; Rectory; Swakeleys
Filkins, Emma 57
Finch, James 80
fire 84
Fitzwilliam, Sir William 17
Flowery Dick 51
football 73
Ford, Fred 59
Ford, George 59
Foreign Office: sports association 23
Forsyth, W. A. 29
Fox and Geese Inn 76-77, **77**, 89
Franklin, William C. 42
French, Percy 61

Geary, James 41
Gell, Charlotte 52-56
Gell, John Henry 52
Gerrards Cross 9
Gibbons, Thomas 46
Gilbey, Arthur N. 20, 21, 63, 69
Gilman, Samuel 40
Gladdy, James 31, 34
Glebe Avenue 88, 89
Glebe Farm 81
Glebe Lane 80, 81
Glebe School 64
Gloucester, Eleanor Duchess of 13
Glover, John 33, 40
golden eagle 69
Goldying, John 44
Goffe, John 39
Goldar, Jabez 46
Goodwyn, Thomas 39
Gordon, Charles G. 34
Gordon, Christina 61
Gospel Oak 10, 69
Gravett, John 43
Gravett, William 43
Great Western Railway 61, 84, 87-89
Gregory, Joseph 80
Grim's Dyke 9

93

Gutteridge Wood 69
gypsies 50, 62, 66-67, 80
Haines, Mark 76
Hall, P. C. Jim 50
Halliwell, William 62
Hamonde, Martha 38
Harefield 9, 24
Harefield Place 28
Harington, Catherine 39
Harington, Sir James 19, 25, 26, 29, 32, 38, 39
Harington, Lucy 39
Harington, William 39
Harrington, Thomas M. 34
Harrison family 41
Harrison, Lancelot 39
Hastings, family 24, 38
Hastings, Katherine 38
Hawkes, Jasper 32
hay 22, 54, 83
haybinding 58
Haydon, Thomas 32
Haynes, W. 39
Haysand, Robert 39
headborough 36, 43, 46
Heathrow 9
Henry VII 17
Herbert, William 38
Hercies Farm 14, 15
Hercies, manor of 13, 14
hermits 47-50
Hetherington, George 40
Heylie, Thomas 38
Hill Farm 58, 84
hillfort 9
Hilliard, George 76
Hillier, William Edward 54
Hillingdon, origin of name 10; parish 13
Hobson, John 18
Hodges, Cyril "Uncle Peter" 63
Hogue, H.M.S. 83
Home Cover 27
Home Farm **14, 15, 77**, 84, 87; dame school 57
Hook, Theodore 76
hot air balloon 81
House of Correction 45
housing 22, 89-91
Howell, Donald 42
Hughes, Walter 68
Humphreys, Leonard 34
Hunt, Rev. John 41

Ickenham, manor of 10, 12, 13, 15, 16, 17-28, 40, 43-46; origin of name 10; parish of 13; — Church of England School 57-64; — County Council School 64; — Cricket Club 72-73; — Debating Society 70; — "Exiles" Cricket Club 73; — Green 41, 49, 76, 80, 87; — Hall **34**, 35, 70; — Halt 87; — High Road 64; — High School 64; — Marsh 80; — St. Giles' Cricket Club 73; — Temporary County School 64;
inns, Coach and Horses 14, 43, **44**, 65, 67, 68, 77, 79, **79**, 88;
Fox and Geese 76-77, **77**, 89;
Soldier's Return 75, 76
Iremonger, Rev. Lascelles 21
Iron Age 9
Isleworth Hundred 46
Ivy House Farm 15
Ivy House Road 72

James, E. J. 42
Jarvis, Maude 62
Jodrell, Henry 40
Joel, George 80
Johnson, Benjamin 46
Jonson, Ben, bust of at Swakeleys 26

Keen, Richard 81
Kelly, Paul M. H. 40
Kendall, Henry 32, 39
Kendall, John, *The sorrows of Ickenham*, quoted 56-57
Kenryke, Henry 38
King, "Ginger" 83
King, James 40
Kingsend United Football Club 73
Kingston, Percy 40
Kinton, William 45
Knightley, Thomas see Charlton, Thomas de
Knightley, William 17

Lambe, Richard 32, 38
Lancasterian School 57
Langton, Rev. Hugh Bannister 31, 40, 70, 73
lantern shows 69-70
Lawrence, Issac 80
Lawrence, Dame Maude 35, 70
Lee, W. A. "Gaffer" 51, 60, 61, 63, 83, 85
Legette, William 43-44
Leofwine, Earl 10
Lethieullier, Benjamin 21
Lewis, Mr. 84
libraries 57, 63
licences 45
Lincoln, Earl of see Clinton, Henry
Little Hillingdon, manor of 17
London Postal Region Sports Club 23
Long Lane 9, 16, 28, 65, 89, 91
Long Lane Farm 16, 46
"Loopy" 51
Lord Mayor, of London 19, 20
Lowe, Rev. F. L. Riches 42
Lowman, Maude Gertrude 59

Mandeville, Geoffrey de 12, 13
Mandeville, William de 12
Manor Farm **15**, 15-16, 81
manorial courts 14, 19, 43-46
marathon races **74**, 75
Markby, Archie 40
Marlowe, John 43
Marriage family 41
Mary, Queen of England 23
Mason, Henry Hewitt 13
Mayor, William 76
Memorial Hall 72
Men's Institute 70-72

mesolithic 9
"Metroland" 90
Metropolitan Railway 87-90
Middlesex Sessions 43-46, 48
Milton, Charlotte 58
Milton Farm 15, 81, 89
Milton, John, bust of at Swakeleys 26
moats 16, 23, 24
Montague, Anne 67, 76
Montague, Ernie 75
Montague, Thomas 76
Montague, William 77, 86
Montgomery, Roger de 12
Moon family 41
More, John 39
Morgage, William 38
Morten, Henry 41
Moss, Thomas 80

Nash, family 63
Nash, George 75
Nash, William 41
Neal, John 80
Nelham, Richard 45
Nelham, Thomas 44, 45
Newdigate family 24
Newdigate, Edward 45
Nicholas, John 19
Nicholls, Nathaniel 38, 39
nonconformists 40-42
Norman, Joseph 80
Norman, Sarah 58
Northolt Airport 58, 84
Norwood, Captain 47

Olympic Games **74**, 75
Orchard Cottage 57, **71**
Osmond, John 45
Osmond, Richard 43

Parish clerk 46
parish council 46
parish registers see St. Giles, Ickenham
Park Clump 28
Parr, Anne, Mrs. William Herbert 38
Partridge, J. A. 10
Paulet, Lady Eleanor 18
Payne, John 39
peace celebrations: world war I 72, 86
Peeche, Sir John 17
Pell, Beauchamp Henry St. John 40, 61, 63
Pell, Beauchamp T. 34, 59
Pepys Close 91
Pepys, Samuel 20, 21
Percy, George 39
Perkins, Jessie 59-60
Pettigrove, Tom 68
Pexall, Anne 18
Pexall, Ralph 17
Pexall, Sir Richard 18
pheasants 69
Philip, John 80
Philipp, John 39
Phillips, John T. 79
Pinn, *River* 14, 28, 69, 87
ploughing **82**
pond 56, **60**, 77

94

Pool, John 81
population 89-90
Post Office 66-67, **67**, 88
prisoners of war 85-86
Providence Congregational Church, Uxbridge 40-42
pump 55-57, **55, 79, 88**
Pynchester 24

Randall family 41
Randell, Tom 86
Ravis, Michael 39
Readinge, Ralph 38
Rectory Field 73, 74-75
Rectory Way 70, 74
recusants 43
Redman, Rob. 39
religious denominations 40-42; *see also* churches
Rikeman, Roger 17
Riordenere, Stephen 39
riots 44-45
roads: Roman 10; new developments 89-91
Roberts, Bob 75
Robinson, Francis 13
Robinson, George 13, 76
Roston, Richard 39
roundabouts: fairgrounds 68; road 91
Royal Flying Corps 84
Russell, Francis 38
Russell, Lord 38

Saich, family 41
Saich, Algernon 46
Saich, Sam 71, 86
"Sailor" 50-51
St. Giles' Church, Ickenham 13, 21, 29-40, **33, 35**, 54, 63, 88, **88**, 90, 91; bells 30-31; font 30, **30**, 34; memorials 32-33, 34, 36-37, **36**; parish registers 37-39; rectors 39-40; restoration 29, 34, 37, 75
St. Margaret's Church Uxbridge, lecturer 39
Sawier, John 40
Say, Edward 32
Say, John 32
Say, Robert 32, 39
Say, Thomas William 32
Say, William 18, 29, 31, 45; memorial 31
Saye, Ann 38
scarlet fever 61
Schools, Abbotsfield 64; Breakspear 64; Church of England 57-64; Douay Martyrs Roman Catholic 16, 64; Glebe 64; Home Farm dame 57; Ickenham High 64; Ickenham Temporary County 64; Lancasterian 57; Swakeleys Secondary Modern 64
Semer, Jeremiah 38
Shirley, Thomas 18-19
shooting 58, 62, 68, 81
Shorediche family 13, 15, 34-35; memorials 32

Shorediche, Edmund 18; memorial 32
Shorediche, Helen 18
Shorediche, John 13, 39, 40
Shorediche, Michael 19, 45; memorial 32
Shorediche, Nicholas 13
Shorediche, Richard 46
Shrewsbury, Earl of *see* Montgomery, Roger de
Simmons, "Yorky" 50
Sims, Joseph 46
Sims, King 75
Slattery, Mrs. 63-64
Smith, John 46
Smyth, Thomas 45
Smyth, William 45
Society for the Preservation of Ancient Buildings 22, 57
Soldier's Return Inn 75, 76
Southwell, H. N. 84
Spaget, Daniell 38
Spelthorne Hundred 46
Spygurnell, John 39
Squires, Spencer 75
stag-hunting 68
Stamborowes, John 19
Stent, "Ducky" 69
Stobart, J. C. 63
Stone Age 9
Streater, Robert 26
Strong, Samuel 13
sun, eclipse of 63
Sutton, Harriet Eliza 35
Swalclyve, Robert de 17
Swakeleys **18, 21, 22, 24-25, 27,** 58, 72, 85; house 23-28; manor of 10, 13, 14, 16, 17-28; origin of name 17
Swakeleys Farm 28
Swakeleys House Ltd. 23
Swakeleys Road 10, 14, 27, 52, 65, **74,** 89, **91**
Swakeleys Secondary Modern Girls School 64
Swakeleys Vault 29

Talbot, Humphrey John 23
tanhouse 43
Tappin brothers 77
Taylor family 41
Taylor, Bert 75
Taylor, Samuel 80
tennis 73-74
Thornhill, Clara 15
Thornhill, Randolph Clarke — 15, 21, 87
Thornhill, Thomas Bryan Clarke — 15, 30
Thorp, John de 39
Ticca 10
tile kilns 28
Toki 10-11
tramps 50-51
Truesdale, Frances 14
Turner, John 43, 46
Turner, Thomas 46
Turner, Wenefred 38
Turner, William 35, 46
Tutankhamen 54
Tykenham, manor of 13

Ulsi 10
United Reformed Church 40-42, **40;** ministers 42
United States Air Force 91
Uxbridge, origin of name 10; — Market House 56; — Rural District Council 87; — Savings Bank 14; — Urban District Council 46, 80; — Volunteer Fire Brigade 85

Vesey, Thomas 39
Viatores, *Roman roads in the south east,* 10
village hall 64, 72
Vincent, Matthew 45
Vyner, Robert 19-21, 32
Vyner, Thomas 21; memorial 32

Wakefield, Robert 39
Walford, Edward *Greater London* (1893) 25
Walter, Richard 19
Waters, Elizabeth 43
Watson, Joseph 80
Weatherley family 41
Weatherley, Anne 80
Weatherley, Henry George 46
Weeden, Charles 54
Weeden, George 46
Weeden, John 46
Weeden, Kenneth M. 34, 85
Weeden, Reginald 46, 71, 73
West Drayton, origin of name 10
West Lodge 28
West Ruislip Air Base 90-91
West Ruislip Station 87
Western Avenue 89
wheelwright 78
Wight, Wulward 10
Wilden, Francis 80
Wilden, Harry 71, 86
Wilden, Montague E. 34
William the Conqueror 12
Willis, E. A. 42
Wilson, Anne 57-59
Winch, Arthur "Punch" 85
Winch, Charley 75
Winch, James 14
Winch, Jane 57
Winchester, John 45
Winchester, Marquess of 18
Wiskin, Nance 86
Wolfe, John 39
Wood, Llewellyn "Woody" 68, 77-79, **78,** 86
Woodley, Philip 49-50
Woodman, Ben 63
Woodman, William 62
Woodstock Drive 90
World War I 22, 34, 54, 63, 68, 72, 83-87
World War II 23, 72, 90
Wright, Edmund 19, 24-25, 26, 27
Wright, William 39
Wulfheard 10
Wynburne, Victor B. 40

Yeading Brook 80
Yonge, Joan 38

95